THE
TITANIC
POCKETBOOK
A Passenger's Guide

NAVAL INSTITUTE PRESS
Annapolis, Maryland

~ **Contents** ~

Preface

This guide is a conceit in which the reader will, I trust, delight, but an imaginative one such as could have been given to a passenger on board the RMS *Titanic* of the White Star Line on her maiden voyage from Southampton Docks on 10th April 1912, to be read at leisure during the Atlantic crossing. Probably the best-known ship in the world, *Titanic* holds an enduring fascination for millions. Much has been written about her, but this pocket book sets out to present the ship as those who built *Titanic* had envisaged her – namely, as the most luxurious liner in the world, providing a quality of service that coined an expression still used today to describe the superlative: 'White Star service'.

Conceived to outclass the competing ships of White Star Line's main rival, Cunard, *Titanic* nonetheless faced stiff competition on the transatlantic route – offering first class accommodation across the Atlantic for those rich enough to afford it (a first class ticket equates today to about £64,000), along with second and third class passage. Even third class passengers (or 'steerage', as they were still referred to) enjoyed perquisites that other shipping lines only offered to second class passengers: linen, wooden panelling in the cabin (albeit with six sharing), the opportunity of a shower (shared), and a dining room (with common tables) offering decent fare. And the financial contribution of third class passengers was critical to the profitability of the transatlantic trade route.[1] The White Star Line, it is estimated, carried as many as two million emigrants across the Atlantic to North America, mainly from Ireland and Scandinavia.

Titanic was built for comfort, not speed. In this respect she followed her predecessors – the first White Star Line ship to follow this rationale was the stunning *Oceanic (II)*, commissioned in 1899 by Thomas Ismay. White Star ultimately left the Blue Riband accolade (awarded for the fastest transatlantic crossing) to its rivals, primarily because ship hull design at the time was such that any speed over 20 knots could only be achieved by logarithmically increasing the horsepower of the engines, with consequent cost increases in engine construction and coal consumption.

Parts One and Two account for the design, construction and launch of the ship. It is helpful to note that *Olympic* and *Titanic* were practically identical as built, the only discernable difference being the screen added to the forward first class promenade deck, which gave *Titanic* a more modern look than her sister. Thus, in reading the descriptions of the time, what went for the *Olympic* externally went for the *Titanic* too, although a very large number of internal alterations were made as a result of the experience gained from building *Olympic* first. Both ships were constructed in Belfast by Harland and Wolff, the leading shipbuilders of the age, innovators in marine engineering design and known for their insistence on the best of fittings for their ships.

The White Star Line had a cosy relationship with Harland and Wolff, whose chairman Lord Pirrie was also a shareholder in White Star Line. They would build three luxurious liners, the *Olympic*, *Titanic* and *Britannic* (originally *Gigantic*) on a 5 percent cost-added basis. A brilliant naval architect, Thomas Andrews, who was also managing director of Harland and Wolff and a nephew of Lord Pirrie, worked on the plans while Alexander Carlisle oversaw the interior fittings and various equipment – including the boat davits for launching the lifeboats at sea – although he left the firm in 1910 to become a shareholder in Welin Davit & Engineering Company Ltd, the firm making the davits. Funding was provided by the American financier J.P. Morgan and his International Mercantile Marine Co., which had taken control of the White Star Line. *Titanic*'s keel was laid down on 31st March 1910 and her hull launched on 31st May 1911. Two slipways were specially constructed to take *Titanic* and *Olympic* as was a novel crane design with two vast gantries. *Titanic* was designed with an overall length of 883 feet 9 inches (269.1 metres), a maximum breadth of 92 feet (28 metres), gross registered tonnage of 46,328 tons and a height from the waterline to the boat deck of 59 feet (18 metres).

Part Three looks in detail at the passenger facilities. These attracted the cream of Edwardian society and it was naturally de rigueur to publish a list of first class passengers who were quite prepared to forego a little speed for the prestige and comfort of travelling by White Star Line. They would nonetheless expect to arrive in New York from Southampton, Cherbourg and Queenstown (Cobh) in six days, as opposed to Cunard's Blue Riband-winning passages of four days seventeen hours. The White Star ships' engines produced a steady 20 knots for an economic use of coal, giving a good power to weight ratio and a more comfortable ride than the vibration-ridden quadruple-screw Cunarders.

Social attitudes of the time were still bound up in the class system, although the impact of the First World War would change this dramatically. Everyone was expected to know their place in society and this was reflected in the rigid delineation between first, second and third class on board – a system familiar in railway travel, too. To an extent this separation remained evident even in the organisation for abandoning the sinking ship after the fateful iceberg collision. But it is the passenger facilities that show this social split most clearly, with the magnificent first class grand entrance and staircases and options of a dining saloon, restaurant, verandah cafés and palm courts, a sumptuous reception room, lounge and smoking room in which to spend time, along with leisure activities offered through Turkish baths, swimming baths, a squash racket court and gymnasium (all inconceivable three decades ago in sail or combined sail and steam ships). In addition, the wealthiest passengers enjoyed en suite and special staterooms. Contrast this with third class accommodation of a dining saloon with long canteen tables, a 'general room', smoking room and accommodation in innovative staterooms of mostly two or four berths (but up to ten), additional two-berth cabins and open accommodation for 164 'steerage' customers. However, *Titanic*'s and *Olympic*'s standards were so high that even this accommodation was finished with oak panelling and teak furniture.

Some turns of phrase (now long gone) in the descriptions of the ship's fittings make delightful reading. When describing the heating thought is given to the likely cultural differences between say an Englishman and an American travelling from the Deep South who 'frequently requires, and is accustomed to, an amount of heat which to a Britisher is well-nigh unbearable'.[2] Thoughts go to those high-backed all-round chairs in draughty British country piles huddled in front of a fire in winter while the rest of the house remained below freezing. Similarly, who today would have a '"Cairo curtain", elaborately carved to allow

TITANIC.

the light to fitfully reveal something of the grandeur of the mysterious East in a Turkish bath'? Attention to sumptuous passenger décor and facilities even extended to the adoption of differing looks for each public room, be it Louis Quatorze in a state parlour room, Louis Quinze in a special stateroom or Louis Seize style in the first class restaurant. This striving for aesthetic perfection is all the more ironic when placed against other aspects of construction – for example, designing the watertight bulkheads to the height of the waterline only, fitting double bilge keels solely to the side of the hull (and not up the ship's sides) or the provision of twenty lifeboats, enough for only half her complement. To be fair, in this respect her designers complied with the Board of Trade's outdated regulations of 1894, which required sixteen boats, a figure calculated in relation to a ship's tonnage and not her complement.[3] Indeed, most other liners of the day – including those throughout Europe – also had many fewer lifeboats than those required to evacuate all their passengers at one time.

Part Four includes information on navigation and safety features and is thereby not only of interest to the discerning passenger but offers reassurance as to the navigational protocols followed by the ship's master. An atmosphere of confidence and optimism provided the backdrop to *Titanic*'s design. She was described by her designers as 'practically unsinkable', which was soon picked up by the brochure writers and the press who boasted of her as 'unsinkable'. However, the litany of mistakes and unlikely circumstances, one followed by another, that caused her to sink changed this view and the regulations relating to safety at sea were sharply revised in consequence. Board of Trade rules at the time of *Titanic*'s build only required sufficient lifeboats for 1,200 of the 2,500 souls embarked, or even for the 3,600 for which she was licensed. After *Titanic*'s demise new rules to enforce sufficient davits, which would, depending on the length of the ship, take lifeboats for all those embarked were passed with commendable speed and came into force from 1st January 1913.[4]

The *Titanic* was the largest liner to be launched up to 1912, and as such her designers, whilst incorporating the latest concept in collision buoyancy with fifteen watertight bulkheads, did not envisage any accident at sea that would open up more than four watertight compartments. Thus it was only thought necessary to construct them to the upper deck at the forward end of the ship and to the saloon deck at the after end. *Titanic* was designed to cope with a collision at the intersection of any two watertight compartments, but could float with her forward three flooded – or her forward four in calm weather. Andrews boasted (correctly!) that *Titanic* could be cut crossways into three pieces and each piece would still float. The freak sideswipe disaster that ultimately occurred has never happened before or since in recorded maritime history. The *International Regulations for Preventing Collisions at Sea*, which had read that 'every vessel shall, in a fog, mist, falling snow or heavy rain storms, go at a moderate speed', were in consequence amended to include 'or at night in the known vicinity of ice'. An aircraft ice patrol was also inaugurated that has been maintained ever since. The Admiralty chart then in use, number 2508, was quickly revised with suggested tracks for ships plying between Europe and North America redrawn further to the south of Newfoundland and the Grand Banks.

But, of course, no-one at the time knew that the awful tragedy was going to happen. *Titanic* was launched in Belfast on 31st May 1911 to a fanfare of pride and optimism. For her owners the liner represented a lucrative opportunity to strengthen the company's financial position and reward its shareholders. Her design, the same as for her sister ships the *Olympic* and the *Britannic*, was a response to the intense rivalry emanating from the 'other British line', Cunard, but also from America and more especially Germany with the Hamburg-America and the Norddeutscher-Lloyd lines.[5] As the embodiment of Edwardian style, *Titanic*'s beautiful lines had followed an evolutionary progression from designer Alexander Carlisle's earlier beauty, the *Oceanic (II)*, and outshone those of any rival.

The jingoistic rhetoric that trumpeted from the press and media of that time is typified by the White Star Line brochure, which describes the *Olympic* and *Titanic* as not only the largest vessels in the world but asserts that 'they stand for the pre-eminence of the Anglo-Saxon race on the Ocean'; going on to proclaim that '...the strength of a maritime race is represented more by its instruments of commerce and less by its weapons of destruction than was formerly supposed'. Consequently, 'these two Leviathans add enormously to the potential prosperity and progress of the race, and the White Star Line have well deserved the encomiums that have been showered upon them for their enterprise and foresight in the production of such magnificent vessels.' Another publicity brochure writes of 'Patriotism and pride that indicate the supremacy of the Anglo-Saxon race leading to an orderly, secure and peaceful world'. It is clear that the passenger of 1912 was not spared the trial of advertising that we take for granted today, although its style and content now seems almost refreshingly naïve, lacking the psychological guile that is used routinely in modern marketing. Contemporary press releases also mentioned the public pride that was invested in the ship and the interest she had generated. This would have given many White Star Line passengers a great deal of confidence before they boarded *Titanic* to cross the Atlantic.

No-one was to know that the maiden crossing was also to be the ship's last. The demise of the *Titanic* was shocking and tragic, but it was also just an unfortunate accident; apportioning blame is a product of the application of hindsight combined with ignorance of the customs of the day.

John Blake FRIN, 2011

John Blake is a former naval officer and navigator, who also directed the licensing of the UK Hydrographic Office archives. A Fellow of the Royal Institute of Navigation, he is the author of The Sea Chart *(Conway, 2004) and* Sea Charts of the British Isles *(Conway, 2005).*

Notes

1. Titanic: Fortune and Fate, *The Mariner's Museum (1998) p51*

2. The Shipbuilder, *Vol. VI, 'The White Star Liners* Olympic *and* Titanic
– Special Souvenir Number', Ed. A. G. Hood (1911) p105

3. The Birth of the Titanic, *Michael McCaughan (1998) p179*

4. The Shipbuilder, *ibid. p148*

5. Building the Titanic, *Rod Green (2009) p20*

WHITE STAR LINE

NEW YORK
PLYMOUTH
CHERBOURG
SOUTHAMPTON

NEW YORK
QUEENSTOWN
LIVERPOOL

BOSTON
QUEENSTOWN
LIVERPOOL

MONTREA
QUEBEC
LIVERPOO

NEW YOR
AZORES
MEDITERRANE

BOSTON
AZORES
MEDITERRANE

United States & Royal Mail Steamers

Part One
INTRODUCTION

The unique position occupied by Messrs Harland & Wolff in the shipbuilding world is due to many causes, but if we were asked to name that which in our opinion was the most potent we should not hesitate to declare for the personal element. Personality has undoubtedly been responsible for the high reputation which the firm possesses ... not only has it the services of an able and experienced staff, but at the head of affairs is Lord Pirrie, a wonderful personality whose influence pervades the establishment from end to end. Under his guiding hand the business has steadily grown to its present pre-eminent position as the premier shipbuilding and engineering establishment in the world. On a site without natural advantages, where all the fuel and material required have to be imported, he has raised up a colossal concern which gives employment to between 14,000 and 15,000 men, and pays out in wages over £25,000 a week... The Olympic successfully completed her trials the same day that the Titanic was launched (May 31 last), and no man, even at the zenith of his career, could hope for greater distinction that Lord Pirrie, the designer and builder of these magnificent vessels, has gained by their production ... In conclusion it would be difficult to name a firm that has done more for the development of commerce than Messrs Harland & Wolff ... the firm have, by their work, exercised a potent influence upon the strengthening process which is knitting the units of the British Empire more closely together, and by this same forging of new commercial links they have done much to bring into a closer band of union the great Anglo-Saxon race.

- Syren & Shipping, 28 June 1911

~Olympic & Titanic~

The advent of these Leviathans of the Atlantic coincides very appropriately with the most important development of modern times – the movement of the British and American people towards the ideal of international and universal peace. Of all the forces contributing to this great and desirable consummation, commerce has been one of the most potent, and as the growth of international trade is largely due to the progress in shipping, it is impossible to over-estimate the service rendered to the Anglo-Saxon race by the enterprise of our Ship-owners and Shipbuilders. No better instance of this spirit of enterprise can be produced than the building of the White Star Liner *Olympic* and her sister ship *Titanic*, constructed as they have been side by side at Messrs Harland & Wolff's Ship Yard, Belfast. The spectacle of these two enormous vessels on adjoining slips, representing over 100,000 tons displacement, was altogether unprecedented, and naturally the public interest taken in the vessels on both sides of the Atlantic has been very keen. It has been felt that, great as the triumphs have been in the past in Naval Architecture and Marine Engineering, these two vessels represent a higher level of attainment than had hitherto been reached; that they are in fact in a class by themselves, and mark a new epoch in the conquest of the Ocean, being not only much larger than any vessels previously constructed, but also embodying the latest developments in modern propulsion.

- White Star Line publicity brochure, May 1911

THE CONSTRUCTION AND GENERAL FEATURES OF THE SHIP.
—— LEADING DIMENSIONS

Dimensions.	
Length over all...	882' 9"
Length between perpendiculars...	850' 0"
Breadth, extreme...	92' 6"
Depth, moulded, keel to top of beam, bridge deck ...	73' 6"
Total height from keel to navigating bridge...	104' 0"
Gross tonnage...	45,000 tons.
Load draft...	34' 6"
Displacement...	60,000 tons.
Indicated horse-power of reciprocating engines...	30,000
Shaft horse-power of turbine engine...	16,000
Speed...	21 knots.

THE SHIPBUILDER.

A Quarterly Magazine devoted to
The Shipbuilding, Marine Engineering and Allied Industries.

Edited by A. G. HOOD.

VOL. VI.   MIDSUMMER, 1911.   SPECIAL NUMBER.

~The White Star Line~

The completion of the immense liner *Olympic*, to be followed very shortly by
her sister *Titanic*, the largest ships in the world, adds yet another triumph of
shipbuilding and engineering skill to the splendid list of vessels built for the
Atlantic passenger service. In no other trade have such remarkable developments taken place in the size of ships and in the comfort and luxury provided
for passengers. Competition between the shipping companies has been very
keen, and efforts to secure pre-eminence have been quickly followed by the
endeavours of rival lines to "go one better". In this respect the White Star Line,
or more properly the Oceanic Steam Navigation Company, has always been in
the first rank since the Company was formed in 1869, and the building of the
Olympic and *Titanic* makes it evident that the characteristic policy of enterprise
and foresight is being worthily maintained.

EARLY HISTORY The White Star flag was flown originally by a line of sailing
vessels founded about 1850, and mainly engaged in the Australian trade to cope
with the great rush to the newly found Australian goldfields. In 1867 the owner
of this line retired and the fleet passed into the hands of the late Mr. Henry
Thomas Ismay. Mr. Ismay commenced by introducing iron instead of wooden
sailing ships; but having had some experience of steamships and Atlantic traffic

as a director of the National Line, he realized the advantages to be obtained by the establishment of a high-class service of steamships in the Atlantic passenger trade, and in 1869 formed the Oceanic Steam Navigation Service for this purpose. In 1870 Mr. Ismay was joined in the management of this Company by Mr. William Imrie, the title of the managing firm being altered to Ismay, Imrie & Co. An order was immediately placed with Messrs. Harland & Wolff to build a new fleet, thus commencing that connection between owners and builders which has been maintained with such marked success up to the present day, all the subsequent vessels of the White Star Line, with the exception of the *Cretic*, having been built at the famous Belfast yard.

THE FIRST OCEANIC The pioneer vessel of the new Line, the first *Oceanic*, was launched at Belfast in August, 1870, and arrived in the Mersey in February, 1871. She was 420 ft. long, 41 ft. broad, and 31 ft. deep, with a tonnage of 3,707, and she embodied a number of improvements previously unknown in the Atlantic trade. Her propelling machinery consisted of two sets of four-cylinder compound engines supplied by Messrs. Maudslay, Sons and Field, of London, working on a single shaft. Each set consisted of two 41-inch diameter high-pressure cylinders and two 78-in. diameter low-pressure cylinders, with a stroke of 60 in. Steam was supplied by 12 boilers, having in all 24 furnaces, and working at 65lb. pressure. The speed of the vessel was about 14 knots with a coal consumption of 65 tons per day.

NOTABLE VESSELS Following the *Oceanic* came a long list of notable vessels, as will be seen from the diagram showing the progress of White Star steamers. Specially noteworthy were the *Britannic* and *Germanic*, built in 1874 and 1875. These vessels had a speed of over 16 knots, and reduced the time of passage to less than 7 ½ days. The *Germanic*, with new engines and boilers, made the passage in 6 days, 21 hours, 3 minutes, in August, 1896. No further development in the direction of high speed was attempted by the White Star Line until, in 1899, they placed on service the successful 20-knot vessels *Teutonic* and *Majestic*, their first twin-screw steamers, both of which, almost up to the advent of the *Olympic*, have been regularly employed between Southampton and New York, the *Teutonic* having been transferred to the Company's Canadian service from Liverpool in May last.In 1899 an important stage was reached by the completion of the second *Oceanic*, a vessel surpassing in dimensions any-thing previously attempted and the first ship to exceed the *Great Eastern* in length. No attempt was made in her design, however, to emulate the high speed attained by the contemporary Cunard and German record breakers. It was considered that a speed of 20 knots was sufficient to make the vessel a reliable seven-day boat, and in this respect she amply fulfilled expectations. Following the *Oceanic*, a return was made to slower speed vessels of 16 to 17 knots, but the increase in size was maintained. The largest vessel of the line prior to the completion of the *Olympic* was the *Adriatic*, built in 1907, her dimensions being 709 ft. 3in., by 75 ft. 6in., by 56 ft. 9in., and speed 17 knots. The completion of the *Olympic* and *Titanic* bring up the total number of White Star liners to thirty-one, having an aggregate gross tonnage of about 460,000.

LATER HISTORY Other notable events in the history of the Line have been the transference, in 1907, of the main service – Liverpool, Queenstown, and New York – to Southampton, Cherbourg, Queenstown and New York, and the passage of its control to the International Mercantile Marine Company, of which the White Star Line forms the most important unit. In 1909 their first entry was made into Canadian traffic with the steamers *Laurentic* and *Megantic*, the largest vessels which have yet been employed in this service. The *Laurentic* and *Megantic* are further notable on account of the fact that whereas the *Megantic*

The first "Oceanic" (1871), pioneer vessel of the White Star Line.

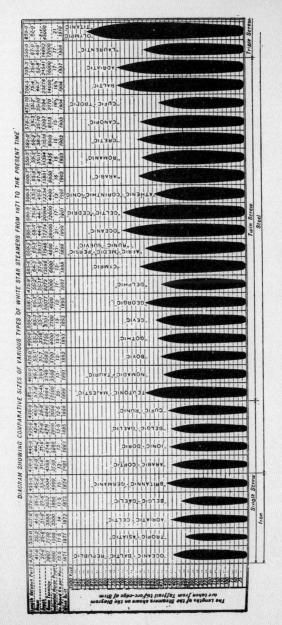

Diagram showing development in size of the White Star Liners.

is propelled with twin screws driven by reciprocating engines, the *Laurentic*, although otherwise of similar dimensions and form, is provided with triple screws and machinery combining two sets of reciprocating engines with a low-pressure Parsons turbine. This experiment was made in order that the relative merits of the two systems of propelling machinery could be ascertained. No results have been published regarding the performances of these ships, but the fact that it was decided to adopt the combined type of engines for *Olympic* and *Titanic*, after the full experience of the two systems secured in this way, is significant.

MANAGEMENT The present chairman and managing director, Mr. Joseph Bruce Ismay, is the eldest son of the founder of the White Star Line, the late Mr. Thomas Ismay, and has occupied that position with great ability since the death of his father in 1899. Mr. Bruce Ismay was born in 1862. He was educated at Harrow and then served a seven years' apprenticeship in the office of Messrs. Ismay, Ismie & Co., after which he proceeded to New York as agent for the White Star Line. Returning later to Liverpool, he was admitted a partner in the firm. Training and temperament alike have combined to fit Mr. Ismay eminently for the position of vast responsibility he holds, and the success of the *Olympic* is in no small measure due to the interest and initiative he has displayed in dealing with the many problems involved. Associated with Mr. Ismay in this work mention should be made of those officials of the Line who have devoted great ability and untiring energy to the mass of detail connected with the building of the two latest and greatest Atlantic liners.

CONCLUSIONS The *Olympic* and *Titanic* are not only the largest vessels in the world; they represent the highest attainments in Naval Architecture and Marine Engineering; they stand for the pre-eminence of the Anglo-Saxon race on the Ocean; for the "Command of the Seas" is fast changing from a Naval to a Mercantile idea, and the strength of a maritime race is represented more by its instruments of commerce and less by its weapons of destruction than was formerly supposed. Consequently, these two Leviathans add enormously to the potential prosperity and progress of the race, and the White Star Line have well deserved the encomiums that have been showered upon them for their enterprise and foresight in the production of such magnificent vessels.

It is safe to predict that the *Olympic* and *Titanic* will enhance the great reputation already enjoyed by the line; they are without a peer on the ocean; though

Mr. Joseph Bruce Ismay.

so large, they are beautiful, alike in their appearance and in the simplicity of the working arrangements. Everything on board has been well – in many cases brilliantly – conceived and admirably carried out, and passengers will find comfort, luxury, recreation and health in the palatial apartments, the splendid Promenades, the Gymnasium, the Squash Racquet Court, the Turkish Baths, the Swimming Pond, Palm Court Verandah, etc. Moreover, the Staterooms, in their situation, spaciousness and appointments, will be perfect havens of retreat where many pleasant hours are spent, and where time given to slumber and rest will be free from noise or other disturbance. Comfort, elegance, security – these are the qualities that appeal to passengers, and in the *Olympic* and *Titanic* they abound.

The horse has been described as the noblest work of the Creator; a ship may be said to be one of the finest of man's creations; and certainly the *Olympic* and *Titanic* deserve special recognition as the product of man's genius and enterprise. A ship – if the Ark can be so designated – played an important part in the early stage of man's development. To-day ships are amongst the greatest civilizing agencies of the age, and the White Star Liners *Olympic* and *Titanic* – eloquent testimonies to the progress of mankind, as shown in the conquest of mind over matter – will rank high in the achievements of the 20th century.

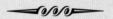

~The Builders of the "Olympic" and "Titanic"~

The builders of the *Olympic* and *Titanic*, the celebrated firm of Harland & Wolff, Limited, have had unrivalled experience in the construction of large passenger vessels, and the new White Star liners but add another triumph to the many which they have to their credit. Unlike many shipbuilding firms, Messrs. Harland & Wolff may be termed builders in the most complete sense of the word. As in the case of all vessels built by them, not only have they constructed the hulls of the *Olympic* and *Titanic*, but also their propelling machinery, while much of the outfit usually supplied by sub-contractors for ships built in other yards has been manufactured in their own works.

White Star Docks, New York, c.1905.

The late Sir Edward J. Harland.

EARLY HISTORY The magnificent shipbuilding yards and works existing at Queen's Island to-day afford little indication of their humble beginnings at the middle of the last century. The site upon which they stand is in reality artificial land, reclaimed by the Belfast port authority during the years 1841-6 while the straight cut to Belfast Lough and the sea, known as the Victoria Channel, was in course of construction. A portion of this ground was enclosed for a shipyard by the Harbour Commissioners in 1847, and was first leased to the firm of Robert Hickson & Co., who commenced to build iron sailing ships there in 1853. To this firm Mr. (afterwards Sir) Edward James Harland came from the Tyne as manager in 1854, when only twenty-three years of age. At first he encountered great difficulties both with the workmen and with the financial affairs of the firm, difficulties which would have daunted a man less determined; but Mr. Harland was no ordinary man, and his personality triumphed over all obstacles. In 1859 Mr. Hickson retired, and Mr. Harland, with the financial assistance of a friend, Mr. G. C. Schwabe, of Liverpool, acquired the yard on his own account. His first contract was for three steamers for the Bibby Line, each 270ft. long by 34ft. wide, by 22ft. 9in. deep, a large order for those days. Thus commenced a business connection which has lasted until the present time, for the latest Bibby liner, the *Gloucestershire*, a fine vessel of about 8,100 tons gross, left Belfast the day after the *Olympic* was launched. The drawing office was placed in charge of Mr. G. W. Wolff, who later was taken into partnership, the firm from the 1st January, 1862, being known as Harland & Wolff. The business prospered exceedingly, the energy and enterprise of the partners, together with the high class work turned out, gradually building up the great reputation which the firm ultimately acquired.

LORD PIRRIE In 1874 Mr. W. J. Pirrie (who was raised to the peerage in 1906) was admitted a partner. In 1895 Sir Edward Harland died, in 1906 Mr. Wolff retired, and Lord Pirrie has remained in supreme control, worthily maintaining the traditions of the firm. The business was turned into a private limited liability company in 1885, the capital being £600,000, divided into six hundred shares of £1,000 each.

Lord Pirrie's career, which has already been the subject of a special article in *The Shipbuilder**, has been one of the most notable among those of the great captains of industry. Entering the Queen's Island in 1862 as an apprentice at the comparatively early age of fifteen, he became successively draughtsman, assistant manager, sub-manager, work manager, partner, and ultimately chairman of Harland & Wolff, Limited. His activities have not been confined to shipbuilding, and his business abilities have secured for him the chairmanship of several leading shipping companies, besides directorships in numerous large industrial concerns.

Associated with Lord Pirrie in the management of the Queen's Island establishment are five directors, each having his own special department to control.

Plan of the Queen's Island Works.

THE PRESENT WORKS The present works are very extensive and employ over 14,000 men. Their extent and arrangement are shown [opposite]. It will be seen that there are no less than eight building slips, all capable of taking large vessels. Nos. 2 and 3 slips were specially laid out for the construction of the new White Star liners in the space previously occupied by three slips, the great increase in the size of the two vessels necessitating a reduction in the number of berths. The ground in way of the new slips was piled throughout and covered with concrete, in some places as much as 4ft. 6in. thick, reinforced by as framework of steel. The floor of the berths is laid at ³⁄₈in. per foot declivity.

WORKSHOPS Electric power and light are supplied to the whole of the works from the firm's own magnificent power station, which has a capacity of no less than 4,000 kilowatts and close upon 7,000 indicated horse-power, the connected motor load exceeding 10,000 horse-power, while for arc lighting along 1,500 additional horse-power is required. In order to deal with the ironwork of the largest vessels, the platers' shed adjoining slips nos. 2 and 3, was largely re-modelled and equipped with the most up-to-date machines while the slips were under re-construction, and here most of the ironwork of the *Olympic* and *Titanic* has been prepared. The sections of the vessels were laid down to full size and moulds prepared for the workmen in the mould loft. In joinerwork – one of the most important items in a large passenger vessel – Messers. Harland & Wolff stand unsurpassed, and possess admirable facilities for dealing with all classes of vessels. The large joiners' shop is shown below.

The same remark regarding facilities also applies to the engineering section of the works, which is exceedingly well arranged. One of the most important shops is the boiler shop, which is 820 feet long by 160 feet broad, with a wing 455 feet long by 90 feet broad. Adjoining the engine works is the quay at which vessels lie while their machinery is being put on board. In the case of the *Olympic* and *Titanic*, however, owing to their size, this berth could not be utilized, and the machinery was put on board the ships by a 200-ton floating crane owned by the firm.

It will be evident from this brief description how completely equipped the Queen's Island establishment is for dealing with the construction of the two immense vessels for the White Star Line.

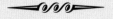

WHITE STAR LINE
TRIPLE SCREW STEAMER
882½ FT.
LONG
"OLYMPIC"
46,359
TONS

Part Two
DESIGN, CONSTRUCTION & LAUNCH

The evolution of the Atlantic liner of to-day has been one of the most remarkable achievements in the scientific progress and commercial activity of modern times. It is difficult to realize that only 73 years have elapsed since the Atlantic was first crossed by a vessel continuously under steam power. This pioneer steamer, the *Sirius*, was a small wooden paddle steamer 208ft. long overall and 178ft. along the keel. Her breadth was 25ft. and depth of hold 18ft. Upon her first Transatlantic voyage, in April, 1838, she carried 94 passengers and averaged about 7 knots speed. What a contrast to the present-day *Kronprinzessin Cecilie*, *La France*, *Lusitania*, *Mauretania*, *Olympic*, and *Titanic*, to mention but the most celebrated of recent ships!

It is impossible in the short space of this article to trace all the stages of development from the *Sirius* to the two latest White Star liners, and only the most important facts can be mentioned. The increase in size and speed has been continuous, as will be seen from Table I, giving the particulars of notable Atlantic liners, and also from the diagram on page 17, which shows the development of White Star ships. The use of wood as the material for construction of the hulls was followed by the introduction of iron, which in turn was superseded by steel. Paddle wheels as a means of propulsion were abandoned in favour of the screw propeller driven by reciprocating engines. The reciprocating engine developed from the compound to the triple, and later to the quadruple-expansion type, two sets of engines, driving twin screws, being adopted as larger powers were

TABLE I.—LARGE ATLANTIC LINERS.

Name.	Builders.	Date.	Length.	Beam.	Depth.	Draught.	Displacement.	Gross Tonnage	Engines.	I.H.P.	Speed.
			Ft.	Ft. in.	Ft. in.	Ft. In.	Tons.				Knots
Great Eastern	Scott Russell	1858	680	83 0	57 6	25 6	27000	24360	Pad. & Sc.	7650	14·5
Paris and New York	Clydebank Works	1888	528	63 0	41 10	23 0	13000	10499	Recip.	20600	21·8
Teutonic and Majestic	Harland & Wolff	1890	565	57 6	42 2	22 0	12000	9686	Do.	19500	21·0
Fürst Bismarck	Vulcan Co., Stettin	1891	503	57 3	38 0	22 6	10200	8000	Do.	16412	20·7
Campania and Lucania	Fairfield Co.	1893	600	65 0	41 6	23 0	18000	12500	Do.	30000	22·01
St. Louis and St. Paul	Cramp, Phil.,U.S.A	1895	536	63 0	42 0	26 0	16000	11629	Do.	18000	21·08
Kaiser Wilhelm der Grosse	Vulcan Co., Stettin	1897	625	66 0	43 0	28 0	20880	14397	Do.	30000	22·5
Oceanic	Harland & Wolff	1899	685	68 5	49 0	32 6	28500	17274	Do.	27000	20·72
Deutschland	Vulcan Co., Stettin	1900	662·9	67 0	44 0	29 0	23620	16502	Do.	36000	23·5
Kronprinz Wilhelm	Do.	1901	663 o.a.	66 0	43 0	29 0	21300	14908	Do.	36000	23·5
Kaiser Wilhelm II.	Do.	1903	678	72 0	52 6	29 0	26000	19361	Do.	38000	23·5
La Provence	Chantiers de Pen-hoët, St. Nazaire	1906	597	64 7½	41 8	26 9	19160	13750	Do.	30000	22·05
Kronprinzessin Cecilie	Vulcan Co., Stettin	1907	678	72 0	52 6	29 0	26000	19400	Do.	38000	23·5
Adriatic	Harland & Wolff	1907	709	75 6	56 9	...	40790	24541	Do.	16000	17
Lusitania	Clydebank Works	1907	760	88 0	60 0	...	44060	30822	Turbines	70000	25·5
Mauretania	Swan, Hunter, & Wigham Richardson, Ld.	1907	760	88 0	60 6	...	44640	31938	Do.	70000	26·0
La France	Chantiers de Pen-hoët, St. Nazaire	1911	685	75 5	52 10	29 6	27000	23000	Do.	45000	23·5
Olympic and Titanic	Harland & Wolff	1911	850	92 0	64 3	...	60000	45000	Recip. & Turbine	46000	21

required. The highest perfection of this type of engine was reached in the German record breakers *Kaiser Wilhelm II* and *Kronprinzessin Cecilie*, which have twin screws and four sets of engines, two sets being mounted on each shaft.

Turbine propelling machinery in conjunction with triple screws appeared on the Atlantic in 1904, when the Allan liners *Victorian* and *Virginian* entered upon service, and was also adopted for the Cunard liner *Carmania*, completed in 1906. The greatest triumphs of the turbine have been won by the quadruple-screw express Cunarders *Lusitania* and *Mauretania*. But although the turbine has been eminently successful for the high-speed ship, at more moderate speeds its economy is not so marked, a fact which has led to the introduction of the latest type of propelling machinery, the combination of reciprocating engines with a low-pressure turbine. When considering the type of machinery to be adopted for the *Olympic* and *Titanic*, the White Star Line and Messrs. Harland and Wolff, as already mentioned, agreed to test the merits of the combination system compared with reciprocating engines of the ordinary type by building two vessels exactly similar except in regard to propelling machinery. These two vessels, the *Megantic*, fitted with reciprocating engines, and the *Laurentic*, fitted with combination engines, were completed in 1909. Their relative performances in the White Star Line's Canadian service completely justified the expectation regarding the superior economy of the combined type of machinery, and it was decided to adopt combined engines for the later and much larger vessels.

~Factors of Design~

It may not be out of place at this stage to briefly indicate the many problems which beset the designer of an Atlantic liner and the main considerations determining the dimensions, form, and arrangement of ships like the *Olympic* and *Titanic* which are intended to eclipse earlier vessels. The two most important factors of design are the speed and passenger accommodation to be aimed at, and it has always been the endeavour of the competing steam-ship companies on the Atlantic to possess vessels which excel in one or both of these respects. Both factors are favoured by increase in size of ship; hence the tendency to greater dimensions which has been so marked during the past few years. The maximum possible dimensions of a new vessel depend upon the dock and harbour accommodation available when the ship is completed; and it is for this reason that Lord Pirrie, among others, has devoted so much time and energy to the question of increased dock and harbour facilities.

Reverting to the subject of speed, high speed is a very costly requirement, not only owing to the great initial cost of the propelling machinery and the heavy cost of fuel in service, but also on account of the necessary fineness of the ship, which limits the earning power as regards cargo carrying and the extent of passenger accommodation. In a high-speed Atlantic liner, the difficulties of design are greatly increased, as the designer is handicapped by the limited draught of water available at the terminal ports, and very careful consideration has to be given to the question of weight, any saving which can be effected being of great value. If, on the other hand, a more moderate speed is aimed at, the problem of weight is much simplified, as the vessel can be built to a fuller model and a greater displacement secured, without exceeding the draught available. It has been the custom of the White Star Line to strive for pre-eminence in passenger accommodation in conjunction with a speed which can be obtained without too great a sacrifice of cargo capacity, and the *Olympic* and *Titanic* have been designed in accordance with that policy. Although a passenger on one of these vessels will not have the honour of crossing in the fastest ship on the Atlantic, he will have many compensating advantages as regards increased comfort at sea and the greater extent and variety of the accommodation provided.

Other matters which require the careful consideration of the designer are the problems of strength, stability, and behaviour at sea. The subject of the strength of an Atlantic liner was ably dealt with by Professor J. Meuwissen in a former special number of *The Shipbuilder*,* and those interested in the technical aspect of the question are referred to that article. As regards stability, while the metacentric height must be sufficient to prevent the vessel taking an unpleasant list when subjected to a beam wind, it should be kept within moderate limits to ensure easy rolling in a seaway. Metacentric heights of from 1ft. 6in. to 2ft. 6in. have been found satisfactory in this respect. Close attention must also be given to the problems connected with watertight subdivision, steering, ventilation, heating, electrical equipment, and the hundred and one items which go to make the complete ship and the magnitude of which will be better realized by the general public from a perusal of the following pages. Enough has been said, however, to indicate that the task of the naval architect in the production of two such vessels as the *Olympic* and *Titanic* is no light one. Indeed the design and construction of these two magnificent ships would have been beyond the range of possibility but for the cumulative experience available from earlier efforts during the past half-century.

* Mauretania *Number, 1907.*

~Building of the Hulls~

THE FOLLOWING ARE THE LEADING SIZES OF THE OLYMPIC AND
TITANIC AS CONSTRUCTED: — DIMENSIONS.

Dimensions.	...
Length over all...	882' 9"
Length between perpendiculars...	850' 0"
Breadth, extreme...	92' 6"
Depth, moulded, keel to top of beam, bridge deck...	73' 6"
Total height from keel to navigating bridge...	104' 0"
Load draught...	34' 6"
Gross tonnage...	45,000 tons.
Indicated horse-power of reciprocating engines...	30,000 hp
Shaft horse-power of turbine engine...	16,000 hp

A comparison of the foregoing information with the table of dimensions of
other vessels given in the preceding section will show that the *Great Eastern*
was 170 feet shorter and 20,600 gross tons less; the *Kaiser Wilhelm II* and
the *Kronprinzessin Cecilie* are each 172 feet shorter and 25,600 tons less; the
Adriatic 141 feet shorter and 20,500 tons less; and the *Mauretania* 90 feet
shorter and about 13,000 tons less.

STRUCTURAL DESIGN The structural design of the *Olympic* and *Titanic* is
comprised as follows. There are eight steel decks amidships – the boat deck,
promenade deck (A), bridge deck (B), shelter deck (C), saloon deck (D), upper
deck (E), middle deck (F), and lower deck (G) – while an extra deck, the orlop,
is fitted, along with a lower orlop deck at the ends of the ship, making ten
decks in all. The main structure of the vessels ends at the bridge deck, which
is carried for 550 feet amidships. To raise the ends of the ships well above
the waterline without having recourse to a large sheer, a poop 106 feet long
and a forecastle 128 feet long are provided. Above the bridge deck, the deck-
house sides and deck plating are of lighter scantling and have two expansion
joints, one forward and one aft, to prevent heavy stresses coming upon the
thin plating in a seaway. The main scantlings have been determined by Messrs.
Harland and Wolff's long experience with large vessels. Material is massed at
the upper flange of the equivalent girder by making the bridge and shelter
deck plating and sheer strakes of great thickness and fitting doubling at these

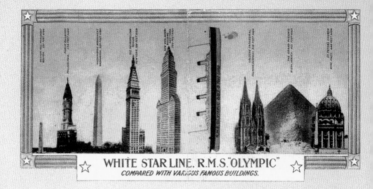

WHITE STAR LINE. R.M.S. "OLYMPIC"
COMPARED WITH VARIOUS FAMOUS BUILDINGS.

points, while the lower flange is strengthened by doubling the bilge plating. The material used throughout is mild steel. The keel of each vessel is formed by a single thickness of plating 1½ in. thick and a flat bar 19½ in. wide by 3in. thick. The bottom plating is hydraulic riveted up to the bilge, the strakes being arranged clincher fashion for this purpose; and the frame bottoms are joggled to avoid the use of tapered packing pieces. To reduce the number of butts and overlaps to a minimum, plates of large size are adopted. The shell plates generally are 6 feet wide and about 30 feet long, with a weight of 2½ to 3 tons. The largest shell plates are 36 feet long and weigh 4¼ tons each.

A cellular double bottom extending right out to the ship's sides, with floors on every frame, is fitted throughout each vessel. This double bottom is 5ft. 3in. deep, and is increased to 6ft. 3in. in the reciprocating engine room. The subdivision of the double bottom into separate tanks is arranged to provide ample facilities for trimming the vessel or for correcting any list due to unequal disposition of coal or cargo. The double bottom is divided into four compartments transversely by the watertight centre keels and watertight longitudinals on each side 30ft. from the centre line, the subdivision being completed in the usual manner by transverse watertight floors. The subdivision into four tanks transversely is also of benefit to the stability of the ship, owing to the limited width of the free water surfaces in the tanks used for the boiler feed water and for the passenger water services. Besides the continuous tank girders mentioned above, there five intercostal tank girders amidships on each side of the centre keelson, and additional girders are fitted beneath the engine rooms.

The spacing of the frames is 3ft. amidships, reduced to 24in. forward and

27in. aft. The frames are of 10-in. channel sections, except at the extreme ends, where a built section of frame and reverse bar is adopted. Web frames 30in. deep are fitted on every third frame (9ft. apart) in the boiler and turbine rooms, and on every second frame (6ft. apart) in the reciprocating engine room. The channel frames extend from the tank top to the bridge deck, some of these bars having a length of about 66ft. and weighing nearly one ton. The beams of the main structure are also of channel section 10in. deep amidships, the largest being 92ft. long and weighing $1\frac{1}{4}$ tons. The beams are connected to the frames by bracket knees. The transverse strength is also maintained by the watertight bulkheads, of which there are fifteen in all, and a number of nonwatertight bulkheads forming the cross bunker ends. The decks have a camber of 3 inches.

The beams of the bridge, shelter, saloon, and upper decks amidships are supported by four longitudinal girders, which are in turn carried by solid round pillars spaced 9ft. apart. Below the middle deck in the boiler rooms round pillars are also adopted, 9ft. apart, in conjunction with strong beams carried across at the lower deck level in way of each web frame. In the case of the inner rows the pillars are spaced out so that they do not interfere with the working passage. In the engine rooms and holds the pillars below the middle deck are wide spaced and of circular built section, the deck girders being increased in strength to suit the longer span. As the ship gets narrower at the ends the number of rows of pillars is reduced.

Bilge keels 25in. deep are fitted for about 300ft. of the vessel's length amidships, to minimise rolling in a seaway.

The two decks forming the superstructure of each ship and the navigating bridge are built to ensure a high degree of rigidity. At the sides they are supported on built-up frames in line with the hull frames, but at wider intervals. The deckhouses are specially stiffened by channel section steel fitted in the framework; and where, as on the boat deck, the public rooms pierce the deck, heavy brackets are introduced to increase the resistance to racking forces when the ship is steaming through a heavy seaway. The boat and promenade decks are increased to 94ft. wide, to enlarge the promenade space. All exposed decks are sheathed with wood, but inside deckhouses and on all decks not exposed to the weather Harding's Litosilo is adopted as the deck covering. This Litosilo was supplied by Messrs. C. S. Wilson & Co., of Liverpool, some 40,000 square yards being required for each vessel.

The "Olympic" Plated and the "Titanic" Framed.

RIVETING Some idea of the great importance of the riveting in the *Olympic* and *Titanic* will be gathered from the fact that there are half a million rivets in the double bottom of each vessel, weighing about 270 tons, the largest rivets being $1\frac{1}{4}$ in. diameter; while in each ship when completed there will be something like three million rivets, weighing about 1,200 tons. To ensure the best workmanship, hydraulic riveting has been adopted whenever possible. Nearly the whole of the double bottom, including the bottom shell plating up to the turn of the bilge and the topside shell and stringer plates and doublings, have been riveted by hydraulic power. The seams of the bottom plating are double riveted, and of the topside plating treble and quadruple riveted. The butts of the bottom plating are overlapped and quadruple riveted, as are also the butts of the side plating, except in the way of the topside shell and doublings, where double straps are adopted.

STEM & STERN CASTINGS As each vessel has triple screws, the stern frame is provided with a boss and aperture for the centre or turbine propeller; while the wing or reciprocating propeller shafts are carried by boss arm castings, round which the shell plating is carried to form 'bossing' of Messrs. Harland and Wolff's improved type. All these castings have been supplied by the Darlington Forge Company, and are of Siemens-Martin mild cast steel, with the exception of the rudder stock which is of forged ingot steel. Some idea of the immense size of the stern castings will be obtained from the particulars of their dimensions and weights given in the following table :-

WEIGHTS & DIMENSIONS OF CASTINGS:

Castings.	...
Stern frame (two pieces)...	70 tons.
After brackets (two pieces)...	73¾ tons.
Forward brackets (two pieces)...	45 tons.
Rudder (six pieces)...	101¼ tons.
Stem bars...	7¼ tons.
Stem connection piece to keel...	3½ tons.
Stern-frame.	...
Height ...	67' 0½"
Length of keel-post...	37' 4"
Section of gudgeon-post...	21' x 13"
After brackets.	...
Centres of shafts...	38'10¾"
Diameter of bosses...	5' 2¼"
Forward bracket.	...
Centres of shafts	38' 5 "
Diameter of bosses	6' 2"

The stern frame is of dished section, 18 in. by 11in., increased to 21 in. by 11 in. solid in way of the aperture, and is in two pieces connected by specially designed scarphs. The total height is 68ft. 3in. and length 37ft. 4in. A large palm is provided at the forward end to form a strong connection to the after boss arms and the main structure of the vessel. The scarphs are connected with best Lowmoor iron rivets 2in. diameter, there being 59 rivets in the forward and 53 rivets in the after scarph, with a total weight exceeding one ton. The great care exercised in fitting these to ensure a strong connection is suggested by the fact that they were all turned and fitted and specially closed with rams.

The after boss arms are in two pieces, connected at the centre line of the vessel by strong deep flanges to form a continuous web right across the ship. This web, again, is riveted to a 2-in. steel plate of special quality, extending from side to side of the vessel. The immense castings are securely attached by means of rivets to the stern frame, shell plating, floors, and framing of the ship. The centres of the wing shafts are 39ft. at the after brackets, and the bosses are 4ft. 10 in. diameter. The introduction of the forward brackets as a means of increasing the strength of the ship at this part is noteworthy. In this case also the two arms have been made in separate pieces and connected by bolts at the centre line of the ship, the whole being securely attached to the ship's plating and framing.

The rudder is of solid cast steel, built in five sections and coupled together with bolts varying from $3\frac{1}{2}$ in. to 2in. diameter. The rudder-stock is of forged steel $23\frac{1}{2}$ in. diameter, and was made from a special ingot of the same quality as used for gun jackets. On the completion of the forging an inspection hole was bored through the stock of the rudder in order to ensure that there were no flaws. The length overall of the rudder is 78ft. 8in., and width 15ft. 3in. The pintles are 11 in. diameter, of hard steel, and are arranged each to take their own proportion of the rudder weight, bearing upon hard steel discs inside the stern post gudgeons. A special feature is that the bottom of the rudder is so arranged that screw jacks can be employed for lifting it in dry dock. The stem bar is of the usual rolled section, and is connected by a steel casting to the centre keelson and keel of the ship. A special feature is the cast-steel hawsepipe attached to the upper portion of the stem bar, to take the steel wire hawser provided for use with the central bower anchor. The weight of this casting is $6\frac{1}{4}$ cwt.

WATERTIGHT SUBDIVISION The watertight subdivision of the *Olympic* and *Titanic* is very complete, and is so arranged that any two main compartments may be flooded without in any way involving the safety of the ship. There are fifteen transverse watertight bulkheads extending from the double bottom to the upper deck at the forward end of the ship, and to the saloon deck at the after end – in both instances far above the waterline. The room in which the reciprocating engines are placed is the largest of the compartments, being 69ft. long, while the turbine room is 54ft.

long. The boiler rooms are generally 57ft. long, with the exception of that nearest the reciprocating engine compartment. The holds are 50ft. long.

The watertight doors giving communication between the various boiler rooms and engine rooms are arranged, as is usual in White Star vessels, on the drop system. They are of Messrs. Harland and Wolff's special design, of massive construction, and are protected with oil cataracts governing the closing speed. Each door is held in the open position by a suitable friction clutch, which can be instantly released by means of a powerful electro-magnet controlled from the captain's bridge, so that in the event of accident, or at any time when it may be considered advisable, the captain can, by simply moving an electric switch, instantly close the doors throughout and make the vessel practically unsinkable. Each door can also be closed from below by operating a lever fitted in connection with the friction clutch. As a further precaution floats are provided beneath the floor level, which, in the event of water accidentally entering any of the compartments, automatically lift and thereby close the doors opening into that compartment if they have not already been dropped by those in charge of the vessel.

A ladder or escape is provided in each boiler room, engine room, and similar watertight compartment in order that the closing of the doors at any time shall not imprison the men working inside, but the risk of this happening is lessened by electric bells placed in the vicinity of each door, which ring prior to their closing and thus give warning to those below.

BUILDING STAGES OF THE OLYMPIC The work of both ships has been carried on in a most expeditious manner. The first keelplate of the *Olympic* was laid on December 16, 1908, and by March 10 following the double bottom was all bolted up, and the work of riveting it by hydraulic power well advanced. The whole of the side framing, which was commenced from the stern, was finished by November 20, 1909, and the plating was completed and almost entirely riveted by April 15, 1910. The vessel, as is well known, was launched 20th October, 1910, and practically only seven months have been taken up in the subsequent work of completion. When the dimensions of the ship are remembered, this performance will be recognised as highly creditable to all concerned.

~Completion~

After the launch, the *Olympic* was moored at the new deep-water wharf belonging to the Belfast Harbour Authorities, and a commencement was made with the work of fitting the propelling machinery on board. The 200-ton floating crane belonging to the builders was employed for the purpose.

The *Olympic* was docked on the 1st April 1911, in the new graving dock belonging to the Belfast Harbour Commissioners, which has the distinction of being the largest graving dock in the world at the present time. The responsible task of docking and undocking was accomplished without a hitch. The *Olympic* was completed by the end of May, 1911, the work of fitting out having been finished in just over seven months from the date of launching, a remarkable performance, especially when it is considered that Messrs. Harland and Wolff were also completing afloat during the same time the two White Star tenders *Nomadic* and *Traffic* for use at Cherbourg, and three other liners, as well as preparing for the launch of the *Titanic*. Between 3,000 and 4,000 men were engaged on the completion of the *Olympic*, on board and in the shops, the total number of men employed by the builders at this period being about 14,000.

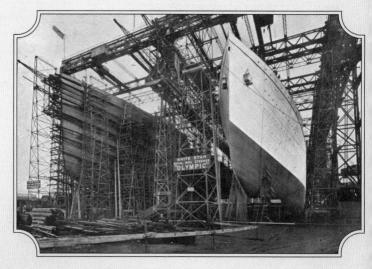

The "Titanic" and "Olympic" on the Stocks.

BUILDING STAGES OF THE TITANIC The progress of the work in connection with the *Titanic* is illustrated by the descriptions of the *Olympic*, the vessels having, as already stated, been built on adjoining berths. It is interesting to note, however, the dates upon which definite stages in the construction of the second vessel were reached. The keel was laid on the 31st March, 1909, or about three months after the *Olympic* was commenced. By the 15th May following the *Titanic* was framed to the height of the double bottom, and was fully framed on the 6th April, 1910, just a year after laying the keel. The vessel was plated by the 19th October, 1910, and was successfully launched on the 31st May, 1911, the launching arrangements being similar to those adopted for the *Olympic*.

THE PROPELLING MACHINERY The combination of reciprocating engines with a Parsons low-pressure turbine, which has been adopted for the propelling machinery of the *Olympic* and *Titanic*, is one of the latest examples of progress in marine engineering. The superior economy of the system is due to the fact that increased power is obtained with the same steam consumption by expanding the steam in the low-pressure turbine beyond the limits possible with the reciprocating engine. Messrs. Harland & Wolff were among the first to see the advantages of the combination arrangement and to put the system to the test of actual experience. This was done in the case of the *Laurentic*, already referred to, and the successful results obtained with this vessel led to the introduction of engines of the combination type in the new White Star liners and other vessels built and building at Belfast.

ARRANGEMENT OF MACHINERY As will be seen from the general arrangement plans of the ships, in the *Olympic* and *Titanic* nearly the whole of the space beneath the upper deck E is occupied by the steam-generating plant, coal bunkers, and propelling machinery. The boiler installation and bunkers occupy six watertight compartments, having a total length of 320 feet. The engine rooms take up a further length of 123 feet, and the electric engine room and shaft tunnels occupy the remaining portion of the ship below the orlop deck. Of the four funnels provided, the foremost three are required for the boiler rooms, while the fourth is used for ventilating purposes and has also built into it the chimney from the extensive galleys.

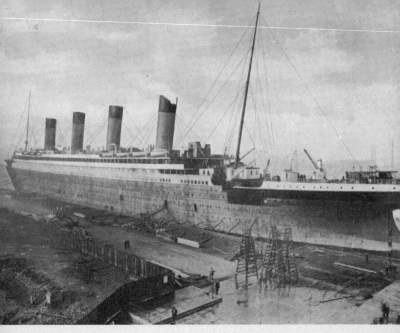

"Titanic" in dry dock at Belfast.

As is well known, the *Olympic* and *Titanic* are triple-screw steamers, each wing propeller being driven by one set of reciprocating engines, and the central propeller by the low-pressure turbine. Owing to the great size of the units, it was found necessary to place the latter in a separate compartment abaft the reciprocating engine room and divided from it by a watertight bulkhead. The reciprocating engine room is placed immediately abaft the aftermost boiler room, and contains, in addition to the main engines, a large amount of auxiliary machinery. In the wings are placed the main feed and hot well, bilge, sanitary, ballast, and fresh water pumps, the auxiliary condenser, the surface heater, and the contact heater, which latter is placed high up in the casing at the centre line; while on the port side space has been found for the extensive refrigerating plant, and on the starboard side for a large engineers' workshop, situated on a flat some distance above the floor level and well equipped with machine tools.

The after engine room contains, in addition to the low-pressure turbine, the main condensers with their circulating pumps, twin air pumps, etc., the evaporators and distilling plant, the forced lubrication pumps with two oil coolers, and a pump for circulating water through them, besides several pumps for bilge and other purposes.

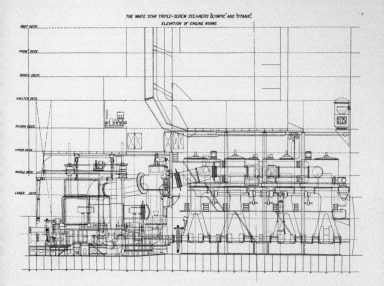

THE WHITE STAR TRIPLE-SCREW STEAMERS 'OLYMPIC' AND 'TITANIC'.
ELEVATION OF ENGINE ROOMS.

Elevation of the ship's engine rooms.

BOILERS Altogether there are twenty-four double-ended and five single-ended boilers in each vessel, designed for a working pressure of 215 lb., which it is anticipated will be maintained under natural draught conditions. The after-most, or No.1 boiler room contains the five single-ended boilers, boiler rooms 2, 3, 4 and 5 contain five double-ended, and the foremost, or No.6 boiler room contains four double-ended boilers. Owing to the great width of the ships, it was found possible to arrange five boilers abreast, except in No.6 boiler room, where, owing to increased fineness, only four abreast could be fitted.

Each of the double-ended boilers is 15ft. 9in. diameter and 20ft. long, and contains six furnaces; while the single-ended boilers, which are of the same diameter as the double-ended but are 11ft. 9in. long, contain three furnaces, so that the total number of furnaces is 159. The latter are all of the Morison type, 3ft. 9in. inside diameter, and are provided with fronts of the Downie 'boltless' pattern. The fire bars are of the Campbell type, supplied by Messrs. Railton, Campbell & Crawford, of Liverpool. The shells of the single-ended boilers are formed in one strake, the double-ended boilers having, as usual, three strakes. All the shell plates are of mild steel 1 in. thick. A view of the boilers arranged in Messrs. Harland & Wolff's works is given overleaf.

The arrangement of uptakes, by which the smoke and waste gases are conveyed to the funnels, is necessarily of a very elaborate nature, no less than twenty branches being required to one funnel in the case of boiler rooms 3 and 4. The branches from adjoining boiler rooms are united immediately above the watertight bulkhead separating the rooms, the bulkhead thus forming a valuable support to the uptakes and funnel above. The four funnels have an elliptical cross section and measure 24ft. 6in. by 19ft. 0in. Their average height above the level of the furnace bars is 150ft. A striking photograph of the last funnel of the *Olympic* leaving the shops is reproduced below.

Boilers arranged in Messrs. Harland & Wolff's Works.

Last funnel of the "Olympic" leaving the Shops.

BUNKER ARRANGEMENTS The arrangements in the *Olympic* and *Titanic* for loading and storing coal and feeding the coal to the stokeholds are the result of great experience. The bunkers consist of a 'tween deck space on each side of the ship between the lower and middle decks, into which the coal is first shipped and from thence distributed into the cross bunkers extending the full width of the vessel in each boiler room. The stokers obtain the coal from doors in the cross bunker end bulkheads at the stokehold level immediately opposite the furnaces, an arrangement which reduces the amount of handling of the fuel for each boiler to a minimum. A further advantage of the bunker arrangement is that no watertight doors are required in the bunker ends, as each set of boilers has the necessary coal supply provided in the same watertight compartment, the watertight bulkheads dividing the boiler rooms being placed at the centre of the cross bunkers.

THE RECIPROCATING ENGINES The two sets of reciprocating engines are of the four-cylinder triple-expansion direct-acting inverted type, balanced on the Yarrow, Schlick and Tweedy system, and are arranged to take steam at 215lb. per sq. in. and exhaust at a pressure of about 9lb. per sq. in. absolute. The cylinders are 54in., 84in., 97in., and 97in. diameter, with a stroke of 75in. in all cases, and each set of engines is expected to indicate about 15,000 H.P. at 75 revolutions per minute. In general design the engines follow the long-tried practice of Messrs. Harland & Wolff. The engine bedplate weighs 195 tons, the columns 21 tons each, and the heaviest cylinder with liner 50 tons. The two low-pressure cylinders are placed one at each end of each set of engines, as is usual with the balancing system adopted, the order of the cylinders, beginning forward, being low-pressure, high-pressure, intermediate-pressure, and low-pressure. Each L.P. cylinder is provided with two slide valves, worked from the same crosshead by a single set of double bar links and eccentrics. The H.P. cylinder is provided with a single piston valve and the I.P. cylinder with two piston valves similarly operated to the twin slide valves on the L.P. cylinders. The valves are operated by Stephenson link motion. The reversing gear for each set is operated by a Brown engine of the usual type, and, in order that the latter may always be at full stroke whatever the cut-off required in the various cylinders, each set of links has its own separate adjustment. Elaborate electrically-operated lifting gear for the cylinder covers, etc., has been necessitated owing to the great weights to be handled, while in addition several electric winches have been provided to deal with the smaller weights. The turning engines are steam-driven.

LOW-PRESSURE TURBINES The low-pressure turbine, which is of the usual Parsons type, will take steam from the reciprocating engines at about 9lb. absolute pressure and exhaust at 1lb. absolute. It is intended to develop about 16,000 shaft horse-power when running at 165 revs. per minute. No astern turbine has been fitted, as the centre shaft is put out of action when the ship is being manoeuvred. The turbine is of immense size, its weight complete being no less than 420 tons. The rotor is 12ft. diameter and 13ft. 8in. long between the extreme edges of the first and last ring of blades. It consists of steel forgings built up in the usual way. The blading is of the Parsons laced type, with distance pieces at the roots and binding soldered on the edge. The blades range in length from 18in. to $25\frac{1}{2}$in. The complete rotor has a weight of about 130 tons. Both hand and motor gear is provided for turning the turbine when under repair. The lifting gear for removing the upper half of the turbine casing is also electrically driven.

SHAFTING AND PROPELLERS The crank and thrust shafts for the reciprocating engines are 27in. diameter with a 9-in. hole through the centre. The line shafting is 26¼ in. and tail-end shaft 28in. diameter with a 12-in. hole through the centre. The crank shaft for each engine weighs 118 tons. There are fourteen collars provided, arranged seven at each end, with space for an intermediate bearing at the middle. Each tail shaft has a loose coupling to facilitate withdrawal outboard for examination. The turbine shaft is 20½ in. diameter, increased at the tail-end to 22½ in., with a 10-in. hole through the centre throughout.

The wing propellers of the *Olympic* are three bladed and have a diameter of 23ft. 6in. The bosses are of cast steel and the blades of bronze. The centre or turbine propeller has four blades and is built solid of manganeze bronze. The diameter in this case is 16ft. 6in.

TELEGRAPHS The engine telegraphs for transmitting orders from the captain's bridge to the starting platform are of the usual type fitted in large vessels and call for no special comment. A system of illuminated telegraphs has been provided between the starting platform and the various boiler rooms to enable the engineer on watch to communicate his orders to each stokehold. With eleven stokeholds to control, the foremost of which is 320ft. from the engine room, the necessity for such an arrangement is evident. Messrs. Evershed & Vignoles, Ltd., of London have provided the transmitters and receivers belonging to the installation. The same firm have also supplied a set of Kilroy's stoking indicators for each stokehold, as well as regulators. The regulator is set to the rate of firing desired by the engineer, and the indicators, which are electrically operated by current switched on from the ship's circuit, give visible and audible intimation to the fireman at the exact moment when each furnace is to be fired. Five indicators are provided in each stokehold, one for each boiler, and are regulated so that the minimum number of furnace doors will be open at the same time, and no opposite doors in a double-ended boiler open together.

WHISTLES The whistles are the largest ever made. Each set consists of three bell domes grouped together with a suitable branch plate. The three domes are

9in., 15in., and 12in. diameter. The total height from the base of the branch piece to the top of the centre dome is 4ft. 2$\frac{1}{2}$in., and the extreme width over the outer dome is 3ft. 6in. The total weight of the three domes and branch pieces is about 6$\frac{3}{4}$cwt. One set has been fitted on each of the two foremost funnels. The whistles are electrically operated, the officer on the bridge having merely to close a switch to give the blast, and there is also an electric time-control arrangement, fitted on the Willett Bruce system, whereby the whistles are automatically blown for 8 to 10 seconds every minute during thick weather.

Part Three
INFORMATION FOR PASSENGERS

The advent of Neptune's latest and greatest conquerors, the White Star Line's huge Triple-Screw Steamers, *Olympic* and *Titanic*, marks an era of advancement in the ocean transportation of passengers. Their surpassing dimensions – exceeding those of any other ships – have made possible the utmost liberality in planning the passenger accommodations, which are upon a scale greater than those of other steamers. Indeed, in comparison with these superb, crowning marine achievements of the Twentieth Century the greatest buildings and memorials of the earth are dwarfed, and in the beauty and comfort of the appointments, combined with the White Star Line's unsurpassed cuisine and service, all the luxuries of the world's best hotels are more than equalled. In the staterooms every wish of the passenger has been anticipated and every "creature comfort" provided, while the public apartments, because of their engrossing beauty as well as their vast area and unusual height, are exceptionally attractive.

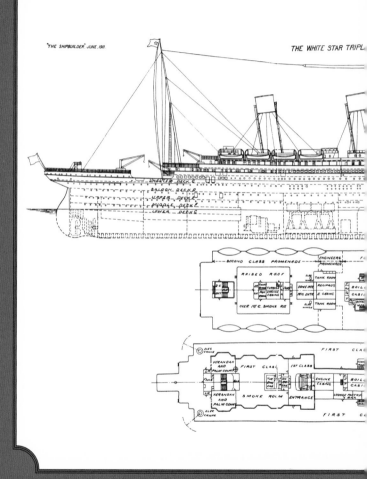

THE WHITE STAR TRIPL

SHELTER DECK C
SALOON DECK D
UPPER DECK E
MIDDLE DECK F
LOWER DECK G

SECOND CLASS PROMENADE
ENGINEERS PROMENADE

RAISED ROOF
TANK ROOM
TURBINE ENGINE CASING
REG. ENTR.
OVER 1ST C. SMOKE RM.
TANK ROOM

FIRST CLASS

VERANDAH AND PALM COURT
FIRST CLASS
1ST CLASS
ENGINE CASING
BOIL
CASI

THE
VERANDAH AND PALM COURT
SMOKE ROOM
ENTRANCE
LOUNGE

FIRST CLASS

MPIC" AND "TITANIC".

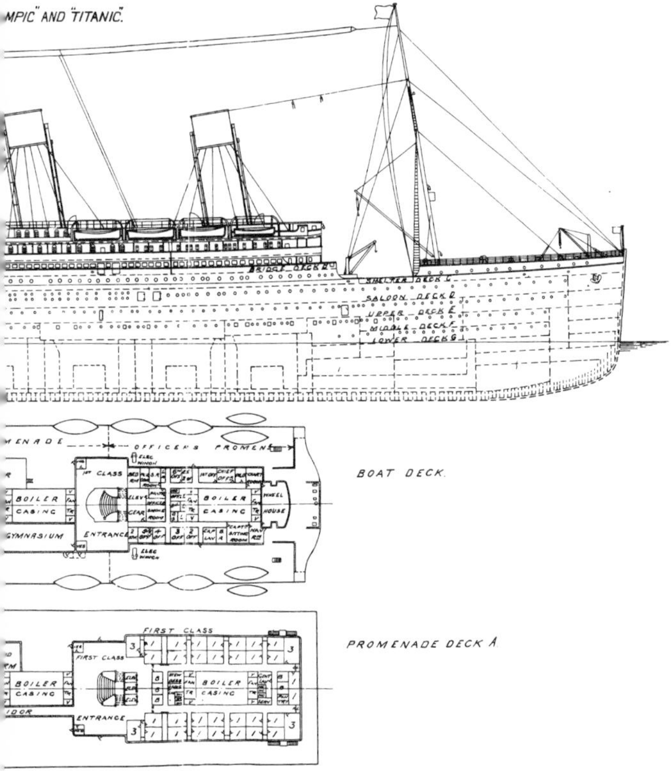
BRIDGE DECK B
SHELTER DECK C
SALOON DECK D
UPPER DECK E
MIDDLE DECK F
LOWER DECK G
OFFICERS PROMENADE
BOILER CASING
GYMNASIUM
ENTRANCE
WHEEL HOUSE
BOAT DECK.
FIRST CLASS
PROMENADE DECK A

THE SHIPBUILDER. JUNE. 1911.

— SOLID SCREEN

— FIRS

POOP DECK

ELEC

CAPSTAN   CAPSTAN

ELECTRIC
CRANE

2ND CLASS PROMENADE

3 3 2 2 2

CRANE

ELEC
WINCH

2ND CLASS
SMOKE
ROOM

2ND CL
ENTR.

RESTAURANT

TURBINE
AND
RECIPRO
ENGINE

PANTRY
GALLEY

4 1

ENGINE
CASING

B

CAPSTAN

CAPSTAN

ELEC
CRANE

ELECTRIC
CRANE

ENTR.

3 3 2 2 2

— SOLID BULWARK —
WITH LARGE WINDOWS Pᴿᴼ

FIRST CL

2 2 2 2 2 2 2 2

BAR

CAPSTAN
GEAR

3ᴿᴰ CL SMOKE
ROOM

3RD CL PROMENADE SECOND CLASS PROMENADE

2ND CL

2 3 3 3 3 3

BAR

GEAR

1ST CLASS

3ᴿᴰ CLASS ENTRANCE

ELEC Nº5

2ND CL

2ND CLASS

BARBER
SHOP

GENERAL
ROOM

ENTRANCE

LIBRARY

ENTR

ENGINE
CASING

B

3 3 3

MAIDS + VALETS SALOON

2 2 2 2 2 2 2 2

4 4

SECOND CLASS

OUTER BAKERS
SHOP

BAKERS
SHOP

1ST CLASS

6 6

3RD CLASS

Nº6

2 2 2 2 2

BAR
HOUSE

FIRST + SECOND

ENGINE
CASING

B

Nº5

ENTRANCE

DINING SALOON

2ND CLASS
PANTRY

ENGINE
CASING

CLASS GALLEY

PANTRY

THIRD CLASS
PERMANENT

2ND CLASS

2 2 2 2
4 4 4 4

1ST CLASS
GALLEY
SCULLERY

3ᴿᴰ CLASS PERMANENT

POTATO
STORE

ENG Nº6

ENGINEERS
MESS

STORE

Nº5

ELECTRIC

ENGINE

ENGINE
CASING

BOILE

CAS

Nº5
LAMP

2ND CL
ENTRANCE

ENGINE
CASING

2 2 2

SECOND CLASS

SECOND CLASS

SE

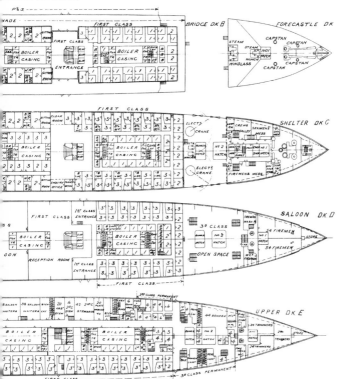

S "OLYMPIC" AND "TITANIC".

BRIDGE DK B   FORECASTLE DK

FIRST CLASS

FIRST CLASS

BOILER CASING

ENTRANCE

BOILER CASING

STEAM   CAPSTAN   CAPSTAN

NO1   STEAM   CAPSTAN

WINCH   HATCH

WINDLASS   CAPSTAN   CAPSTAN

FIRST CLASS

SHELTER DK C

CLOAK ROOM

BOILER CASING

BOILER CASING

CREWS

ELECTS CRANE

ELECTS CRANE

CREWS   GALLEY   SEAMENS MESS

NO2 HATCH

FIREMENS MESS

PANTRY PRINTING OFFICE

FIREMENS MESS

SALOON DK D

FIRST CLASS   1ST CLASS ENTRANCE

BOILER CASING

RECEPTION ROOM

1ST CLASS ENTRANCE

3RD CLASS

OPEN SPACE

FIREMEN

HATCH   NO 2   HATCH

NO 1 HATCH

54 FIREMEN

54 FIREMEN

WC
STORE

FIRST CLASS

UPPER DK E

38 SALOON WAITERS

20 1ST CLASS STEW

42 2ND C STEW

3RD CLASS PERMANENT

44 SEAMEN

BOILER CASING

BOILER CASING

24 TRIMMERS

24 TRIMMERS

2ND STORE

BUNK NO 2   HATCH   HATCH   NO 1 HATCH

36 TRIMMERS

FIRST CLASS

3RD CLASS PERMANENT

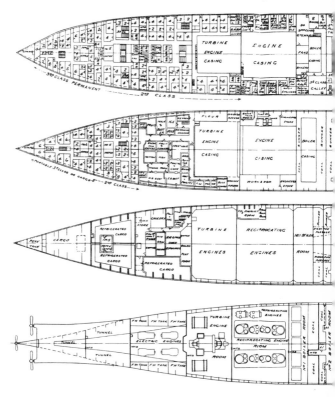

THE WHITE STAR TRIP

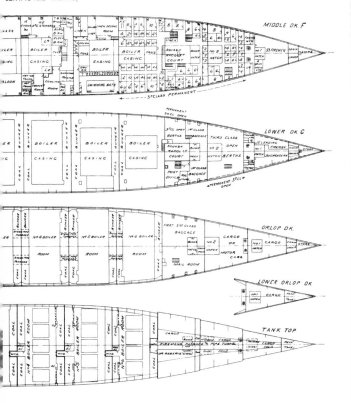

"OLYMPIC" AND "TITANIC".

MIDDLE DK. F

LOWER DK G

ORLOP DK.

LOWER ORLOP DK

TANK TOP

~The Arrangement of the Decks~

There are ten decks in the ship, named from the bottom upwards:- Lower orlop, orlop, lower, middle, upper, saloon, shelter, bridge, promenade, and boat. The passenger decks, promenade, bridge, shelter, saloon, upper, middle, and lower, are named alphabetically A B, C, D, E, F, G. Two of the decks are above the moulded structure of the ship. The lower orlop, orlop, and lower decks do not extend for the complete length of the structure, being interrupted for the machinery accommodation. The bridge deck extends for a length of 550 feet amidships, the forecastle and poop on the same level being respectively 128 feet and 106 feet long. The promenade and boat decks are also over 500 feet long.

The first class passengers are accommodated on the five levels from the upper to the promenade decks. The second class passengers have their accommodation on the middle, upper and saloon decks, and the third class passengers on the lower deck, forward and aft, and on the middle, upper and saloon decks after.

~Passenger Accommodation~

For first class passengers there are 30 suite-rooms on the bridge deck and 39 on the shelter deck. These are so arranged that they can be let in groups to form suites, including bedrooms, with baths, &c., with communicating doors. But on each of these two decks, close to the companion-ways, on either side, adjacent rooms are fitted up as sitting or dining-room.

In all there are nearly 350 first class rooms, 100 of these being single berth rooms. There is accommodation for over 750 first class passengers. For second class passengers the rooms are arranged as two or four-berth rooms, the total number of second class passengers being over 550. For the third class passengers there is a large number of enclosed berths, there being 84 two-berth rooms. The total number of third class passengers provided for is over 1,100.

The arrangement of the passenger accommodation has been very carefully worked out. There is a first class main companion-way at the forward end of the accommodation, extending from the boat deck to the upper deck, with large halls on each level, while further aft is a second companion-way extending from the promenade deck to the shelter deck. There are two second class companion-ways; one extending from the boat deck to the middle deck, and the other from the bridge deck to the middle deck, the second class public rooms being placed between them − viz., the smoke room on the bridge deck, the library on the shelter deck, and the dining saloon on the saloon deck, with the staterooms on the saloon, upper, and middle decks. There are three elevators incorporated in the main companion-way for the first class passengers, and one in the main second class companion-way for the second class passengers. The first class elevators extend from the upper deck to the promenade deck, with entrances at each deck level. The second class elevator extends from the middle deck to the boat deck.

On the boat deck accommodation is provided for the captain and officers, containing smoke room and mess room. Rooms for the Marconi installation are also arranged in the same house, with the wheel-house and navigating bridge adjoining at the fore end. The first class main companion-way ending on this deck has a handsome dome overhead in a spacious entrance, and adjoining this entrance is a large gymnasium fitted out with the latest appliances. It is 44ft. long, by 18ft. wide, by 9ft. 6in. high, and is lighted by eight windows of exceptional size. Here passengers can indulge in the action of horse-riding, cycling, boat-rowing, etc., and obtain beneficial exercise, besides endless amusement. The gymnastic appliances have been supplied by Messrs. Rossel, Schwarz and Co., of Wiesbaden.

Plan of Suite Rooms on 'B' Deck.

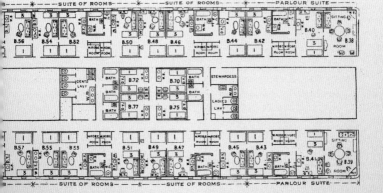

First Class Passenger Elevators [top] – Squash Racquet Court [middle]
– Gymnasium [above].

~Disposition of Rooms, &c.~

On the promenade deck forward are a large number of the single-berth rooms for first class passengers, the reading and writing room, 41' 0" x 41' 0", with the lounge adjoining, 59' 0" x 63' 0", and further aft the first-class smoke room, 65' 0" x 61' 0", with a verandah palm court built in two compartments, each 30' 0" x 25' 0". The bridge deck is devoted very largely to single-berth and suite rooms, with a la carte Restaurant, 60' 0" x 45' 0".

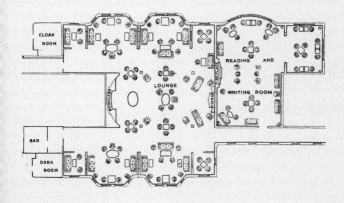

Plan of First Class Lounge and Reading and Writing Room on 'A' Deck.

On the shelter deck there are a great number of first class staterooms and suites, special dining saloons for maids and valets, Marconi and postal officials, and offices in the entrance hall, and, abaft of amidships, the second class library 58' 0" x 40' 0". The third class smokeroom and general room are under the poop on this level.

The saloon deck, as its name suggests, is largely occupied by the dining rooms. Abaft of the grand stairway is a reception room the full width of the ship and 54 feet long, leading into the dining saloon, which is also the full width of the ship and 114 feet long, having seating accommodation for 532. The pantries and galleys are abaft this, and then the second class dining-room, which also is the full width of the ship, is 71 feet long, and has seating accommodation for 394.

First-class staterooms are at the forward end of the main first class companion-way, and are arranged to accommodate one, two or three passengers. The second class staterooms are situated immediately abaft the second class dining saloon, and further aft are the third class staterooms.

Accommodation is provided on the upper deck for first class passengers on the starboard side, in one, two and three-berth rooms, the accommodation for the stewards and restaurant staff being fitted on the port side off the working passage. Second and third class staterooms are also provided on this deck.

On the middle deck is situated the third class dining saloon amidships, extending the full width of the ship, and for a length of 100 feet, with seating accommodation for 473 passengers; the third class galley, pantries, &c., adjoining. At the forward end, convenient to the first class main companion-way, are arranged the Turkish baths, including steam, hot, temperate, cooling and shampooing rooms. Convenient to these are situated two electric bathrooms and also a commodious swimming bath. It is 30ft. long by 14ft. wide, and is fitted out exactly as would be an up-to-date swimming bath on shore. Staterooms for second class passengers are arranged on this deck aft, as well as third class passengers both forward and aft.

Another innovation on board this ship is the provision of a squash racquet court. The court is situated on the lower deck, and extends two decks high for a length of 30 feet. A spectator gallery is placed at the after end of the court on the

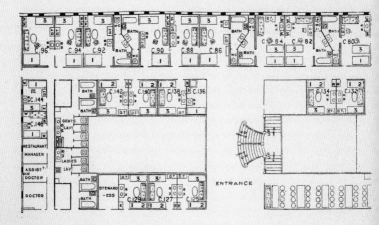

Plan of typical Special Staterooms on 'C' Deck.

The Swimming Bath.

middle deck level. Excellent accommodation for the firemen has been provided at the forward end of the vessel, through the lower, middle, upper and saloon decks, giving access to the boiler rooms by two spiral stairs and a tunnel. The arrangement keeps the firemen entirely clear of the passenger accommodation. The engineers' quarters are on the middle deck, and the mess room, pantries, offices, &c., on the deck above – off the working passage.

~The Decorations~

It is impossible to adequately describe the decorations in the passenger accommodation; the ship must be seen and inspected for these features to be fully appreciated. They are on a scale of unprecedented magnificence; nothing like them has ever appeared before on the ocean. The following brief description of some of the principal rooms, together with the illustrations, will convey some idea of the artistic treatment and luxurious appointment.

Promenade Spaces

The first class promenades on the three top decks in the ships are exceptionally fine. The bridge deck (B deck) promenade is entirely enclosed. It is a magnificent space over 400 feet long, 13 feet minimum width each side of the vessel, and with a solid side screen fitted with the large square lowering windows that constitute one of the most popular features of recent passenger vessels. These windows can be raised or lowered at will, and thus passengers can enjoy the conditions they prefer, having protection from the weather, and at the same time an uninterrupted view of the horizon.

The deck above this, the promenade (or A) deck, is the principal promenade, and is entirely devoted to first class passengers. It is more than 500 feet long and forms a splendid promenade, the width in parts exceeding 30 feet. This is covered by the deck above, but is open at the sides above the bulwark and rail.

The topmost deck – the boat deck – also devoted to first-class promenading, is 200 feet long and the full width of the ship. This deck is surmounted only by the open canopy of heaven.

The spaces assigned for second class promenades are also unusually spacious, and include a length of 145ft. at the after end of the boat deck as well as a covered-in space 84ft. long, with sliding windows at the side, on the shelter deck abreast the second-class library.

The third class passengers have a promenade on the shelter deck in the after well, and a large covered-in space on D deck forward, which is fitted with tables and seats, and can be used in any kind of weather.

First Class Dining Saloon

This immense room has been decorated in a style peculiarly English—that, in fact, which was evolved by the eminent architects of early Jacobean times. It differs from most of the great halls of that period, chiefly in being painted white instead of the sombre oak which the 16th and 17th century builders would have used.

For details, the splendid decorations at Hatfield, Haddon Hall, and other contemporary great houses have been carefully studied, the coved and richly-moulded ceilings being particularly characteristic of the plasterers' art of that time. The furniture of oak is designed to harmonize with its surroundings, and at the same time to avoid the austere disregard for comfort in which our forefathers evidently found no hindrance to the enjoyment of a meal.

Five hundred and thirty-two passengers can dine here at the same time; but as we saunter round the room between the groups of chairs, we see that the semi-privacy of small parties has been carefully provided for: we come to several recessed bays in which families or friends can dine together practically alone, retired from the busy hum of surrounding conversation.

First Class Dining Saloon.

Reception Room

Dignity and simplicity are the characteristics of the reception room. Its beautifully-proportioned white panelling in the Jacobean style, delicately carved in low relief, will indeed make a fitting background to what will probably be the most brilliant mise-en-scene on the ship, for it is here that the Saloon passengers will foregather for that important moment upon an ocean-going ship – *l'heure ou l'on dine* – to regale each other with their day's experiences in the racquet court, the gymnasium, the card-room, or the Turkish bath.

The handsome bronze ceiling lights, or the wall-brackets, will reflect their hundred lights upon the glittering jewels of women in brilliant evening frocks, and the black coats and white fronts of the men gathered round the room. Some of the passengers will stand to gaze at the magnificent tapestry directly facing the staircase, specially woven on the looms at Aubusson, or will await their friends seated upon the capacious Chesterfields or grandfather chairs upholstered in a floral pattern of wool damask, or the comfortable cane furniture distributed at intervals. Upon a dark, richly coloured carpet, which will further emphasize the delicacy and refinement of the panelling and act as a foil to the light dresses of the ladies, this company will assemble – the apotheosis, surely, of ocean-going luxury and comfort. What more appropriate setting than this dignified Jacobean room redolent of the time when the Pilgrim Fathers set forth from Plymouth on their rude bark to brave the perils of the deep!

A reception room has also been provided in connection with the restaurant, consisting of a large and spacious lounge decorated in the Georgian style. Here

Restaurant Reception Room.

friends and parties will meet prior to taking their seats in the restaurant. The elegant settees and easy chairs are upholstered in silk of carmine colour, with embroideries applied in tasteful design. The breadth of treatment and the carefully proportioned panels on the walls, with richly carved cornice and surrounding mouldings, form an impressive ensemble, which is distinctly pleasing to the eye. There is accommodation for a band in this room.

Restaurant

The Restaurant is of the Louis XVI period in design, and is panelled from floor to ceiling in beautifully marked French walnut of a delicate light fawn brown colour, the mouldings and ornaments being richly carved and gilded. In the centre of the large panels hang electric light brackets, cast and finely chased in brass and gilt and holding candle lamps. On the right of the entrance is a counter with a marble top of fleur de pêche, supported by panelling and pilasters recalling the design of the wall panels.

The room is well lighted by large bay windows, which are a distinctive and novel feature, and give a feeling of spaciousness. These are draped with plain fawn silk curtains with flowered borders and pelmets richly embroidered. The windows themselves are divided into squares by ornamented metal bars. Every small detail, down to the fastenings and hinges, has been carried out with regard to purity of style.

The ceiling is of plaster, with delicately modelled flowers in bas relief, forming a simple design of trellis in the centre and garlands in the bays. At various well-selected points hang clusters of lights ornamented with chased metal gilt and crystals.

The floor is covered with a rich pile carpet of Axminster make, and a non-obtrusive design of the period in a delicate vieux rose, which forms an admirable background, and completes the harmonious ensemble.

Comfort has been well considered in the arrangement of the room. It is furnished with small tables, to accommodate from two to eight persons, with crystal standard lamps and rose-coloured shades to illuminate each table.

The chairs have been particularly well studied, and are made in similar light French walnut to the walls, carved and finished with a waxed surface and upholstered with an interesting tapestry representing a treillage of roses in quiet tones assisting the general harmony of colour.

For convenience of service there are several dumb-waiters encircling the

The main staircase.

columns and forming part of the decorative scheme. On one side is ample accommodation for an orchestra, partly recessed and raised on a platform, flanked on either side with a carved buffet, the top part being a vitrine to hold the silver service, and the lower part for cutlery, thus completing the necessities for a well-appointed restaurant to satisfy every requirement.

A Café Parisien, which is an entirely new feature on board ship, has been arranged in connection with the restaurant, and here lunches and dinners can be served under the same excellent conditions and with all the advantages of the restuarant itself. This café has the appearance of a charming sun-lit verandah, tastefully decorated in French trellis-work with ivy and other creeping plants, and is provided with small groups of chairs surrounding convenient tables.

Staircases and Entrances

We leave the deck and pass through one of the doors which admit us to the interior of the vessel, and, as if by magic, we at once lose the feeling that we are on board a ship, and seem instead to be entering the hall of some great house on shore. Dignified and simple oak panelling covers the walls, enriched in a few places by a bit of elaborate carved work, reminiscent of the days when Grinling Gibbon collaborated with his great contemporary, Wren.

In the middle of the hall rises a gracefully curving staircase, its balustrade supported by light scrollwork of iron with occasional touches of bronze, in the form of flowers and foliage. Above all a great dome of iron and glass throws a flood of light down the stairway, and on the landing beneath it a great carved panel gives its note of richness to the otherwise plain and massive construction of the wall. The panel contains a clock, on either side of which is a female figure, the whole symbolizing Honour and Glory crowning Time. Looking over the balustrade, we see the stairs descending to many floors below, and on turning aside we find we may be spared the labour of mounting or descending by entering one of the smoothly-gliding elevators which bear us quickly to any other of the numerous floors of the ship we may wish to visit.

The staircase is one of the principal features of the ship, and will be greatly admired as being without doubt the finest piece of workmanship of its kind afloat.

First Class Lounge.

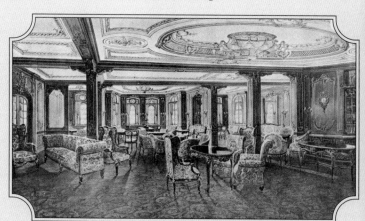

Lounge

The lounge, being a room dedicated to reading, conversation, cards, tea-drinking and other social usages, is decorated in the style which was in vogue in France when Louis XV was on the throne, when social intercourse was the finest of fine arts, and when the Salon was the arena in which the keenest intellects of the age 'crossed swords' and exchanged the most delicate conversational thrust and parry. Now, as then, the British workman is supreme in the production of the finely-carved 'boiseries' with which the walls are covered, and in which, without interfering with the symmetry of the whole, the fancy of the carver has everywhere shown itself in ever varying details.

When talk becomes monotonous, we may here indulge in bridge and whist, or retire with our book or our letters to one of the many quiet retreats which reveal themselves to the thoughtful explorer. The chairs and sofas are so soft and cosy, however, that on them inducements to slumber may easily prevail, to the detriment of our literary efforts.

First Class Smoke Room.

Smoke Room and Verandah

The walls are panelled with the finest mahogany, carved in the taste of our Georgian forefathers, and relieved everywhere with inlaid work in mother-of-pearl. Here, seated around the home-like fire, we may enjoy Mr. Norman Wilkinson's fine paintings of the 'Approach to the New World', which hangs in *Olympic*'s smoke-room, or his 'Leaving Plymouth Harbour', which hangs in *Titanic*'s smoke room; and meanwhile smoke and drink as wisely and well as we feel inclined.

The light comes tempered and softened through the painted windows, where the voyager sees depicted the ports and beauty spots with which he is familiar or hopes to visit, as well as some of the gay and glorious ships which in the past wore so beautiful an aspect, with their low prows and soaring stern-castles.Here, too, are personifications of the Arts – Poetry, Painting, and the like – which have adorned our surroundings and ministered to our pleasures.

Passing through the silently-revolving doors, we emerge upon a gay little verandah, over whose green trellis grow climbing plants, which foster the illusion that we are still on the fair, firm earth; but one glance through the windows, with their beautifully-chased bronze framing, adds to the charm, and we realize that we are still surrounded by the restless sea, once so dreaded a barrier to national intercourse. Set in this flowery arbour are numerous inviting little tables, at which we can take our coffee or absinthe in the open air, much as we do in our own summery gardens on land.

The Cooling Room

The cooling room on the middle deck in connection with the Turkish baths is in many respects one of the most interesting and striking rooms on the ship. The port-holes are concealed by an elaborately-carved Cairo curtain, through which the light fitfully reveals "something of the grandeur of the mysterious East."

The walls are completely tiled, from the dado to the cornice, in large panels of blue and green, surrounded by a broad band of tiles in a bolder and deeper hue.

Cooling room of the Turkish Baths.

The dado and doors and panelling are in a warm-coloured teak, which makes a perfect setting to the gorgeous effect of the tiles and the ceiling, the cornice and beams of which are gilt, and the intervening panels picked out in dull red. From these panels are suspended bronze Arab lamps. The stanchions are cased also in teak, carved all over with an intricate Moorish pattern, surmounted by a carved cap. Over the doors are small gilt domes, semi-circular in plan, with their soffits carved in a low-relief geometrical pattern. As those who partake of Turkish baths are constrained to spend a considerable time in the cooling room, no pains have been spared to make it interesting and comfortable. Around the walls are low couches, and between each an inlaid Damascus table, upon which one may place one's coffee, cigarettes or books.

As the drinking of fresh water is one of the concomitant features of the benefits of taking the bath, there is a handsome marble drinking fountain set in a frame of tiles. There is also a teak dressing table and mirror with all its accessories, and a locker to which valuables may be committed, whilst scattered around the room are innumerable canvas chairs.

Reading and Writing Room

The pure white walls and the light and elegant furniture show us that this is essentially a ladies' room. Through the great bow window, which almost fills one side of the room, we look out past the deck on which our companions in travel are taking the air, over the vast expanse of sea and sky. An atmosphere of refined retirement pervades the apartment; a homely fire burns in the cheerful grate; our feet move noiselessly over the thick, velvety carpet, and an arched opening leads to an inner recess – a sanctuary so very peaceful that here it would seem as if any conversation above a whisper would be sacrilege.

The Reading and Writing Room.

Sitting Room of Parlour Suite, Room B38 (Louis Seize Style).

Bedroom of Parlour Suite, Room B40 (Empire Style).

Suite Bedroom, room B59 (Georgian Style).

Special First Class Stateroom, Room B63.

First Class Staterooms

The finish and decoration of the first class staterooms are well in keeping with the excellence of the public rooms; the staterooms are also exceptionally large and beautifully furnished. Perhaps the most striking are the suite rooms, of which there is an unusually large number, decorated in different styles and periods, including the following :— Louis Seize, Empire, Adams, Italian Renaissance, Louis Quinze, Louis Quatorze, Georgian, Regency, Queen Anne, Modern Dutch, Old Dutch.

Each of the first class staterooms has a cot bed in brass, mahogany, or oak, and in most of the suite rooms the cot beds are 4 feet wide. This is a distinct feature which will be greatly appreciated by passengers.

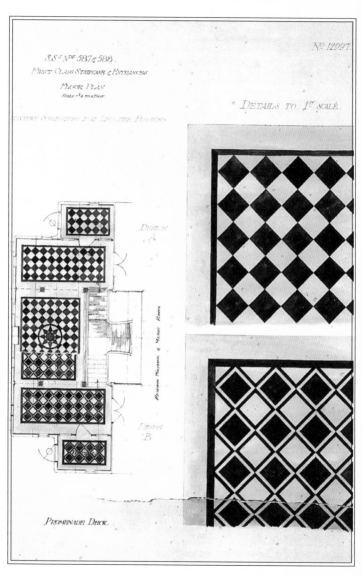

S.S.º Nºˢ 587 & 588.
FIRST CLASS STAIRCASE & ENTRANCES
FLOOR PLAN
Scale ⅛ to a Foot

Nº 12997.

DETAILS TO 1ˢᵀ SCALE.

DESIGN A

DESIGN B

PROMENADE DECK.

Hand-coloured concept drawings produced by the interior designers Heaton Tabb & Co. The First Class staircase and entrances shown here are markedly similar to those used for the White Star Line's "Olympic" class vessels.

WHIT
FLEM
GLA

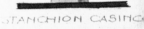

STANCHION CASING

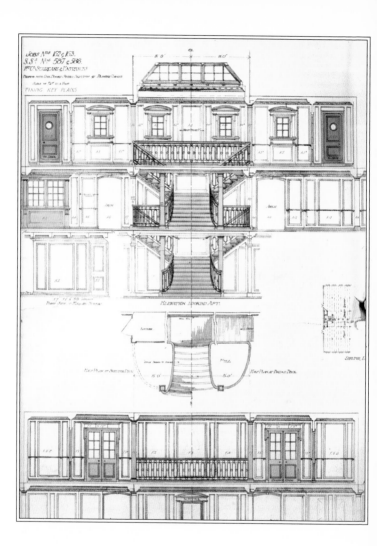

~Second Class Accommodation~

The White Star Line has done much to increase the attractions of second class accommodation during recent years, having made a special feature of this in a number of their vessels; and in the *Olympic* and *Titanic* it will be found that this class of passenger has been very generously provided for. It would have been difficult, a few years ago, to conceive such sumptuous appointments in the second class. Nothing has been omitted in the determination to place the two new White Star leviathans beyond criticism as to the excellence of the accommodation both in the second and third classes.

THE SECOND CLASS DINING SALOON is situated on the saloon deck aft: it extends the full breadth of the vessel, and is an exceedingly fine room, with extra-large opening pivoted sidelights arranged in pairs. The panelling of this room is carried out in oak, the design of which is taken from examples in the early part of the 17th century, with details of a somewhat later period introduced. There is a handsome sideboard extending the full length of the after bulkhead, surmounted with cabinets elaborately carved. At the forward end a specially designed sideboard, with piano in the centre, is provided; the furniture is in mahogany, the upholstery of crimson leather, and the floor has linoleum tiles of special design.

Second Class Dining Saloon.

THE SECOND CLASS LIBRARY is another excellent apartment, with panelling in sycamore handsomely relieved with carvings; the dado is in mahogany and also the furniture, which is of special design, covered with tapestry. A large bookcase at the forward end, the windows at the sides, of large dimensions, arranged in pairs, draped with silk curtains, and the handsome Wilton carpet complete the general comfortable – indeed, luxurious – appearance of the room.

Second Class Library.

SECOND CLASS SMOKE ROOM In this room the decoration is a variation of Louis XVI period; the panelling and dado are of oak relieved with carving; the furniture is of oak of special design, covered with plain, dark green morocco; the floor is laid with linoleum tiles of special design.

The Second Class Forward Entrance and Staircase is handsomely carried out in oak. This staircase is one of the features of the ship, as it extends through seven decks, and an elevator incorporated with the centre of the staircase serves six decks. The Second Class After Entrance and Staircase is also panelled in oak and extends through five decks.

SECOND CLASS STATE ROOMS The majority of these rooms are arranged on the well-known tandem principle, ensuring natural light to each cabin; the rooms are finished enamel white, and have mahogany furniture covered with moquette, and linoleum tiles on the floor.

Second Class State Room [top] – Second Class Deck [above].

SECOND CLASS PROMENADE Needless to say, the spaces provided for second class promenades in this vessel are unusually spacious, and the enclosed promenade is a unique feature which will be fully appreciated by passengers.

~Third Class Accommodation~

The accommodation for third class passengers in these steamers is also of a very superior character, the public rooms being large, airy apartments, suitably furnished, and in excellent positions, and the same applies to the third class staterooms and berths.

THE THIRD CLASS DINING SALOON is situated amidships on the middle deck, consisting of two saloons extending from ship's side to ship's side, well lighted with sidelights, and all finished enamel white; the chairs are of special design. The position of this apartment − i.e., in the centre of the ship − illustrates the wonderful strides made in passenger accommodation in modern times. Third class passengers to-day have greater comfort on the ocean than first class passengers had before the great developments had taken place for which the White Star Line is largely responsible.

THE THIRD CLASS SMOKE ROOM is situated aft on the shelter deck. It is panelled and framed in oak with teak furniture, and is a very suitable and comfortable room. Here, under the soothing influence of the fragrant weed, many a thought will be given to the homeland and those left behind.

Third Class Smoke Room.

THIRD CLASS GENERAL ROOM This is also aft on the shelter deck. It is panelled and framed in pine and finished enamel white, with furniture of teak. This, as its name implies, will be the general rendezvous of the third class passengers – men, women and children – and will doubtless prove one of the liveliest rooms in the ship. The friendly intercourse, mutual helpfulness and bonhomie of third class passengers is proverbial, and, remembering that many of them have arrived at the most eventful stage in their career, we realize that "touch of nature that makes the whole world kin." The new field of endeavour is looked forward to with hope and confidence, and in these vessels the interval between the old life and the new is spent under the happiest possible conditions; in fact, were Mark Tapley on the *Olympic* and *Titanic*, he would find these conditions all too favourable for his fellow-passengers to need the display of his exceptional qualities.

THIRD CLASS PROMENADE To add, as it were, the finishing touch to the excellent provision made for the comfort and well-being of the third class passengers, there is a large apartment arranged under the forecastle as a third class promenade, and fitted with tables and seats, so as to be useful in any kind of weather.

~General Ship's Fittings and Furnishings~

Beds

As already mentioned when describing the first class state-rooms, all the lower berths consist of cot beds in brass, mahogany, and oak, many of them being 4ft. wide. The brass cot beds, which have been supplied by Messrs. Hoskins and Sewell, Limited, of Birmingham, for both the *Olympic* and *Titanic*, are all lacquered by that firm's 'Varnoid' process, which gives a lustre and finish to the brass work unequalled by any other lacquer, and is guaranteed to stand the action of the sea air and sea water. The same firm have fitted their 'Tapex' spring mattresses to all berths throughout the first and second class accommodation, and their 'Orex' spring and chain mattresses to all berths in the third class quarters. They have also supplied the galvanized metallic berths for the open steerage, the portable cabins for the temporary third class, and the whole of the crew's berths.

Kitchen of a large Atlantic Liner fitted by Wilsons.

Culinary Department

No department in a passenger vessel is of more importance to the passengers than that associated with the preparation and service of food, and in no department have greater improvements been introduced during recent years. The difficulty in many ships is to find room for all modern facilities in the limited space allotted to the culinary arrangements. No such disadvantages exist, however, in the *Olympic* and *Titanic*, as the importance attached by the White Star Line to its cuisine has led to the provision of ample space for every requirement, and the culinary departments in these ships are among the most complete in the world.

The first and second class kitchens, serving rooms, pantries, bakeries, sculleries, etc., are situated on the saloon deck between the first and second-class dining saloons, and extend the full width of the ship for a length of nearly 160ft. In the kitchen there are two huge ranges having a frontage of 96ft. and containing 19 ovens, possibly the largest ranges ever made. There are also four silver grills, two large roasters, ranges of steam ovens, steam stockpots, hot closets, bain-maries, and electrically-driven triturating, slicing, potato-peeling, mincing, whisking, and freezing machines.

A new departure has been made in the arrangement of the flues. These are all taken below the deck, the object being to minimize the radiation of heat. This is certainly a step in the right direction, and one likely to be followed in future vessels. A large hoist provides communication between the kitchen department and the cold storage rooms.

A vegetable-preparing room, scullery, coal bunker, and larder, provided with all the latest labour-saving appliances, are conveniently arranged on the starboard side of the kitchen. The bakery, which is in itself worth a visit, is placed just aft of the kitchen on the port side. It contains electrically-driven dough-making and other machines, besides water-tube ovens for turning out the very highest class of Vienna table bread. The confectionery department, adjoining the bakery, is fitted with every conceivable appliance for the modern practice of the confectioner's art.

The pantries and service rooms, which have been arranged with a view to obtaining perfect service of hot and cold food, are situated in close proximity to the dining saloons which they serve. There is nothing so annoying as a semi-cold dinner or luncheon, or the long waits frequently experienced when dining in public places. There need be no fear of such happenings on the

Olympic or *Titanic*. Not a single contrivance for rapid and efficient service has been overlooked. The fittings include bain-maries, hot closets, entree presses, silver coffee apparatus, automatic egg-boilers, milk scalders, electric hot plates, and carving tables of the latest design, all carefully arranged to prevent crowding or confusion among the waiters. The cold pantries or stillrooms are also arranged in the most suitable positions to make the service complete.

A separate kitchen, with its own pantry and scullery, is provided for the restaurant, and adjoins the latter on the bridge deck. Access from the lower kitchen is obtained by means of a spiral staircase extending through two decks. The restaurant kitchen, though not so large as the main kitchen, is equally well equipped. There are also separate pantries attached to the various smoking rooms, buffets, lounges, parlour suites, etc.

The third class galley and pantries adjoin the after end of the third class dining saloon on the middle deck, and are fitted out in a manner which would have been envied by a first class chef some years ago. There is also a large third class bakery. The whole of the cooking apparatus has been supplied by Messrs. Henry Wilson & Co., Limited, of Liverpool, than whom no firm has had greater experience in this class of work.

Service of Plate

The service of plate, which comprises in all about 10,000 pieces, has been supplied by the Goldsmiths and Silversmiths Co., Ltd., of London, a firm who have had great experience with the supply of plate to large hotels. In the case of the *Olympic* and *Titanic* various novel features have been introduced. One of the largest pieces in the service is a massive duck press, which forms a most imposing adjunct. There is also a neat portable spirit lamp, with a quick-heating flame, for keeping warm special sauces and making Turkish coffee. Further novelties are the fruit tymbal and caviar dishes, in which the contents are kept cool by an ice bath when taken from the cold storage and placed before the passenger.

On the waiting tables are electrically heated Rechaud stands of the Goldsmiths Company's special type. One of the advantages of this useful article is that any degree of heat, when once obtained, can be retained by a very small consumption of electricity. Another point which may be mentioned is that all handles, covers, parts, and fittings are interchangeable, an arrangement which greatly facilitates cleaning and general utility.

The cutlery, spoons, forks, and small wares, numbering over 21,000 pieces, and about 3,000 dishes, tureens, and other larger goods, have been supplied by Messrs. Elkington & Co., of Birmingham.

Ventilation and Heating

Ventilation and heating constitute two of the most difficult problems in the arrangement of a large passenger vessel, but the manner in which they have been solved in the case of the *Olympic* and *Titanic* leaves nothing to be desired. Indeed the ventilation and heating system of these vessels is more elaborate and probably more perfect than any yet attempted on board ship. Broadly speaking, in the case of the large third class compartments, the principle adopted is to drive in warm air by means of electrically-driven fans, the air being distributed in all directions through insulated trunks. A pleasant temperature is thus maintained even in the coldest weather.

The ventilation and heating of the first and second class accommodation, on the other hand, involved more special treatment, as the demands of the passengers are so varied. For instance, an American travelling from the Southern States frequently requires, and is accustomed to, an amount of heat which to a Britisher is well-nigh unbearable. With a view to meeting all requirements, after careful thought it was decided to provide an air supply to the passages and individual staterooms which is warmed to a moderate degree, so that an even and pleasant temperature can be maintained. This may be regarded as a warm-air system only, as distinct from a hot-air system, on the 'Plenum' method. Each first class room is also fitted with an electric heater of ample capacity, so that passengers requiring additional warmth can obtain it to the desired extent, while those who prefer a cooler atmosphere are equally well catered for.

In addition to the hot and warm air delivery fans, there have been provided a large number of suction fans for taking foul air from the lavatories, galleys, pantries, and other quarters, so that not only is fresh air brought into the ship, but all vitiated air is removed from those portions of the accommodation which, unless ventilated, might prove objectionable. The fans, of which no less than 64 have been required for the ventilation of the accommodation, are all of the 'Sirocco' type manufactured by Messrs. Davidson & Co., Ltd., and are driven by Allen motors designed in accordance with Messrs. Harland & Wolff's specification. The motors are provided with both hand and automatic control for the variation of speed to suit the particular system of trunks to which the fans they actuate are connected. This is a very necessary provision, as, if the motors always run at the same speed, they are liable to be either overloaded or to fail in the demands made upon them, it being impracticable to determine beforehand the precise speed required in each case.

The mechanical system of ventilation adopted renders superfluous the numerous cowls which encumber the decks of so many liners, these being, in the case of the *Olympic* and *Titanic* – to use an Irishism – 'conspicuous by their absence'. For the same reason the space usually sacrificed for the time-honoured domes over the public apartments is utilized in these vessels for other and more advantageous purposes.

Sidelights and Windows

Natural ventilation and the admission of daylight to the interior of the various rooms have been carefully studied, about 2,000 windows and sidelights altogether. Indeed the numerous sidelights and there being the magnificent array of windows form one of the most striking features of the new ships.

Mention has already been made of the novel arrangement of six and four sidelights adopted in the first class dining saloon and reception room, the oval lights 22in. by 17in. in the first class stateroom, and the sliding windows of the enclosed promenade. A special glass, supplied by the Maximum Light Window Glass Company, of London, has been used for the inner windows of the dining and reception room. By means of the combination of lenses and prisms introduced in this glass, the light from the portholes is dispersed over a greater area than would be the case if ordinary glass had been adopted. All the public rooms situated on the bridge, promenade, and boat decks have windows of exceptionally large size, as will have been observed from the illustrations already given.

Passenger Elevators

The lift service, for which Messrs. R. Waygood & Co., of London, have been responsible, is considerably in advance of that of any previous vessel. The three first class passenger elevators in each vessel are arranged side by side in one trunkway. Each elevator will raise a load of 15 cwt. between the upper and promenade decks, a height of 37ft. 6in., at a speed of 100ft. per minute. The cages are about 5ft. 4in., by 6ft., by 7ft. high, and are made of dark mahogany. Each cage has a glass roof and ventilator, and is furnished with a portable upholstered seat and an electric lamp. The entrance is fitted with a collapsible gate, which is electrically locked and must therefore be closed before the lift can be started.

The winding gear is fitted directly overhead, and is driven by a special slow-speed motor to ensure quiet running. The gear consists of a steel worm and a phosphor bronze worm wheel, enclosed in a cast iron case forming an oil bath. The thrust of the worm shaft is taken by doubleball thrust bearings. The gear is fitted with a winding drum, having two steel wire ropes connected to the cage and two separate ropes for the counter-balance weight. An automatic electric brake comes into action when the current is shut off for any reason. The controller for electric operation is worked by a car switch in the cage, with a self-centring detachable handle. Special provision is made to guard against over running in either direction in case of inattention on the part of the opera-tor or any failure in the controller. The cages are guided by round turned steel runners, in order to give the smoothest possible movement in the lift, and are counter balanced by a cast iron weight working also on round steel runners. A novel feature of the lift service is the provision in the second class accommo-dation of a passenger elevator, also supplied by Messrs. Waygood. This lift is practically identical with the first class passenger elevators, except that the cage is more plainly furnished.

Electric Baths

Two electric bathrooms of the most modern type have been arranged adjacent to the Turkish baths at the middle deck level.

Magneta Clocks

The clocks, of which there are 48 throughout each vessel, have been supplied by the Magneta Time Co., Ltd., and all are actuated electrically on the Magneta system which obviates the use of galvanic batteries. They are controlled by two master clocks placed in the chart room, so that they may work in complete unison and each register exactly the same time. As is well known to ocean trav-ellers, the ship's clocks gain over half an hour each day when going westwards and lose a corresponding amount when returning to Europe. To allow for this difference in time the master clocks are set each day at noon by the officer in charge, who puts them backwards or forwards according to the longitude.

Illuminated Signs and Pictures

A number of electrically illuminated signs are distributed throughout the first and second class accommodation to direct passengers to the respective main entrances and public rooms, while on view in the gymnasium are attractive illuminated multi-coloured pictures of sections of the *Olympic* and *Titanic*, and a map of the world with a network of the many White Star steamship routes which encircle the globe.

Telephone Installation

The telephone installation of the *Olympic* and *Titanic* is divided into two sections, viz . the navigating group and the internal system. All the apparatus is of the very latest type and has been installed on the most approved lines. The navigating group provides for communication between the following:-

The wheel house on the bridge and the forecastle.
The wheel house on the bridge and the crow's nest,
The wheel house on the bridge and the engine room.
The wheel house on the bridge and the poop.
The chief engineer's cabin and the engine room.
The engine room and Nos. 1, 2, 3, 4, 5 and 6 stokeholds.

The instruments employed are Messrs. Alfred Graham and Co.'s patent loud-speaking navy 'phones of the type illustrated [see p. 88]. Except in the chief engineer's cabin, the telephones are of the 'Universal' pattern, by which calls are given by means of an interrupter as well as by voice. The apparatus is mounted in special forms to suit the various positions. On the forecastle and poop the instruments are contained within a polished brass casing mounted on a pillar, and the whole fitting is arranged in portable form, so that the apparatus can be used at two alternative positions in the case of the forecastle set and at a second position on the poop. For the crow's nest the telephone is mounted within a metal hood, and this set also is portable. In the wheel house on the

Loud-speaking telephone.

navigating bridge four instruments are fitted. Each telephone is provided with an indicating device, and, in addition to a flag showing as is usual, a signal lamp is caused to glow upon a call being received. In the engine room three telephones are employed, and the instrument for communicating with the boiler rooms operates in conjunction with a combined switch and indicator giving both lamp and flag signals, as in the case of the bridge instruments. In each boiler room the telephone is mounted within a metal hood, and a special calling receiver is provided at each station, as well as a visual indicator. The telephone in the chief engineer's room is of the cabin type.

The current for operating the system is obtained from the ship's lighting circuit, which is reduced to a pressure suitable for telephonic work by means of resistances, and the noise of commutation, inherent in the machine-generated supply, is eliminated by the introduction of inductance coils. A standby battery is also provided, and is introduced in the circuit, should the main supply fail, by means of an automatic switch.

The internal system provides for intercommunication between a number of cabins through a central exchange. The exchange switchboard has a capacity of 50 lines, the stations connected being a number of first class staterooms and also the rooms of the chief officials and various service rooms. The switchboard is arranged to give a lamp signal upon a call being made, and in addition to the usual audible signal a voice call can be given to the exchange from any station in connection, so that rapidity of operation is assured. The user at one of the cabins has simply to pick up the telephone and say straightaway the station he wishes to speak to and a loud receiver at the exchange gives the instruction.

The operator, seeing a lamp glowing corresponding with the calling station, then connects the calling station with the station required, thus obviating the usual delay in communicating with the calling station and ascertaining the position required. The current supply is obtained from the lighting circuit, as in the case of the navigating telephone system, and the automatic switch and standby battery are contained within the exchange switchboard casing. The telephone sets in each cabin are of Graham's intermediate loud-speaking type [opposite], and comprise a hand set with a circular metal push and terminal box. At the majority of the positions the fittings are silver-plated, and at others of polished and lacquered brass. The wiring of the system has been planned on the most approved principles, and junction boxes have been introduced so as to facilitate testing and extension of the installation.

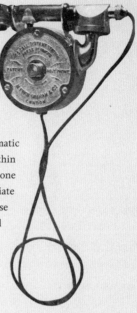

Cabin telephone.

GENERAL INFORMATION FOR PASSENGERS IN THE FIRST CLASS

BREAKFAST from 8 until 10 o'clock.

LUNCHEON at 1 p.m.   *DINNER* at 7 o'clock.

The Bar opens at 8 a.m., and closes at 11.30 p.m.

Lights are extinguished in the Saloon at 11 p.m., Lounge at 11-30 p.m., and Smoke Room at 12 Midnight.

DIVINE SERVICE in the Saloon on Sunday at 10.30 a.m.

SEATS AT TABLE Passengers who have not previously arranged for seats at table to be reserved should apply for same to the Second Steward. Children are not entitled to seats in the Saloon unless full fare is paid.

WIRELESS TELEGRAMS All Southampton–Cherbourg–Queenstown–New York, Liverpool–Queenstown–New York, Liverpool–Quebec–Montreal, Liverpool–Halifax–Portland, and Liverpool–Queenstown–Boston Mail and Passenger Steamers of the White Star Line are fitted with the Marconi system of Wireless Telegraphy, and messages for despatch should be handed in at the Enquiry Office.

AN ENQUIRY OFFICE has been provided for the convenience of Passengers, where all enquiries for information of a general character should be made. Letters, Cables, Telegrams and Marconigrams are received here for despatch, and Postage Stamps can be purchased, and Deck Chairs and Steamer Rugs hired at this office, through which also all Mails will be distributed.

None of the ship's staff other than those on duty in the Enquiry Office are authorised to accept Letters or Telegrams for despatch.

CABLEGRAMS & TELEGRAMS should be handed in at the Enquiry Office an hour before the arrival at any port called at.

THE SURGEON is authorised to make customary charges, subject in each Case to the approval of the Commander, for treating passengers at their request for any illness not originating on board the ship. In the case of sickness developed on board no charge will be made, and medicine will be provided free in all circumstances.

BAGGAGE Questions relating to Baggage should be referred to the Second Steward, who is the Ship's Baggage Master. Trunks, Chairs which Passengers may desire to leave in Charge of the Company, should be properly labelled and handed to the Baggage Master on the Wharf at New York, and such articles will be stored entirely at owner's risk. It is necessary for passengers themselves to see all their Baggage is passed by the U.S. Customs Authorities on landing.

DECK CHAIRS can be hired at a charge of 4/– each for the voyage.

STEAMER RUGS can be hired at a charge of 4/– for the voyage.

PASSENGERS are requested to ask for a Receipt on the Company's Form, for any additional Passage Money, Chair or Steamer Rug Hire, or Freight paid on board.

EXCHANGE OF MONEY The Purser is prepared, for the convenience of passengers, to exchange a limited amount of English and American money, and he will allow at the rate of $4.80 to the £1 when giving American money for English currency, or £1 for $4.95 when giving English money for American money.

The following rates of exchange have also been adopted for American and French and German money – Eastbound, $1 = 5 Francs = 4 Marks; Westbound, Notes and Gold–19 cents per Franc or 23 cents per Mark; Silver–18 cents per Franc or 22 cents per Mark.

PASSENGERS' ADDRESSES may be left at the Enquiry Office in order that any letters sent to the care of the Company may be forwarded.

TRAVELLERS' CHEQUES payable in all parts of Europe, can be purchased at all principal offices of the White Star Line. These Cheques are accepted on board White Star steamers in payment of accounts, but the Pursers do not carry funds to enable them to cash same.

AUTOMOBILE TOURS Arrangements have been made whereby passengers by the White Star Line can hire automobiles to meet them on arrival of the steamer at Queenstown, Liverpool, Plymouth, Cherbourg or Southampton for tours in the British Isles or on the Continent. Orders may be sent from America or Canada through the White Star Line Offices, or direct from the steamer by aid of the Marconi Wireless Telegraph.

This Steamer is fitted with Marconi's system of Wireless Telegraphy and also with Submarine Signalling Apparatus.

WIRELESS TELEGRAM RATES

FOR UNITED STATES The minimum Marconi rate via Seagate, Segaponack or South Wellfleet (Cape Cod), or through the medium of a passing steamer and one of these stations, is 8s. 4d. for ten words. Each extra word 6d.; text only counted; address and signature free; land charges additional; all charges must be prepaid.

The minimum rate via Siasconsett or Cape Race, or through the medium of a passing steamer and these stations is 12s. 6d., for ten words. Each extra word 9d.; text only counted; address and signature free; land charges additional; all charges must be prepaid.

The minimum Marconi rate via Sable Island or Cape Sable, or through the medium of a passing steamer and this station is 16s. 8d. for ten words. Each extra word 1s.; text only counted; address and signature free; land charges additional; all charges must be prepaid.

FOR CANADA The minimum Marconi rate via Quebec, Grosse Isle and Father Point, or through the medium of a passing steamer and one of these stations, is 2s. 1d. for ten words; each additional word 1½ d. The minimum Marconi rate via Clarke City, Grindstone, Fame Point, Heath Point, Harrington, Point Rich, Point Armour, Belle Isle, Cape Ray, or through the medium of a passing steamer and one of these stations, is 4s. 2d. for ten words; each extra word 3d. The minimum rate through the Cape Race station, or through the medium of a passing steamer and this station is 12s. 6d. for ten words; each extra word 9d. The minimum rate via Montreal and Three Rivers, or through the medium of a passing steamer and this station is 1/3 for ten words; each additional word 1d. Text only counted; address and signature free; land line charges additional. All charges must be prepaid.

FOR UNITED KINGDOM. The rate via Crookhaven or other stations in the United Kingdom, or through the medium of a passing steamer, is 10d. per word; every word in address, text and signature counted; land charges additional; all charges must be prepaid.

SHIP TO SHIP The rate from ship to ship is 8d. per word; every word in address, text and signature counted, and all charges must be prepaid.

RESTAURANT In addition to the regular Dining Saloon there is a large modern à la carte Restaurant on Deck B, where meals may be obtained at any time between 8 a.m. and 11 p.m. at fixed charges, as shown on the bill of fare issued from day to day. Passengers wishing to use the Restaurant should apply on board to the Manager for the reservation of seats.

The Restaurant is under the management of the Company, who have appointed Mr. L. Gatti, late of Oddenino's Imperial Restaurant, London, as manager.

If the passage is taken entirely without meals in the regular Dining Saloon, an allowance of £3 per adult will be made off the ocean rate, excepting that on rates of £35 per adult and upwards the allowance will be £5 per adult.

This reduction in fare, however, can only be granted when passengers announce their intention to book without meals, and of making use of the Restaurant, at the time of purchasing their ticket, and no rebate or reduction can be made under any other circumstances.

LOUNGE AND RECEPTION ROOMS These rooms are situated on Deck A and at the entrance to the Main Dining Saloon on Deck D respectively. They are intended for the use of both Ladies and Gentlemen, and afternoon tea and after-dinner coffee will be served, while liqueurs, cigars and cigarettes may be purchased there.

Books may be obtained from the Bookcase in the Lounge on Deck A on application to the Steward in charge. By special arrangement with "The Times" Book Club, a supply of recent works is placed on board each voyage, as a supplement to the permanent collection of standard works.

The Lounge will be closed at 11-30 p.m. and the Reception Room at 11 p.m.

PASSENGER ELEVATORS There are three elevators provided for the use of Passengers, running between Decks A, B, C, D and E.

VERANDAH CAFÉ AND PALM COURT situated on Deck A, where light refreshments are served.

TURKISH, ELECTRIC AND SWIMMING BATHS A fully equipped Turkish Bath is situated on Deck F, consisting of the usual steam, hot, temperate, shampooing and cooling rooms. Electric Baths and a Swimming Bath are also provided in conjunction with same, and experienced attendants will be in charge.

Turkish Baths are available for Ladies from 10 a.m. to 1 p.m., and for Gentlemen from 2 to 6 p.m., tickets being obtainable at the Enquiry Office at a charge of 4/- (or $1) each, which includes the use of the Swimming Bath.

Separate Swimming Bath Tickets can also be obtained at One Shilling, or Twenty-Five Cents, including use of costume.

THE SWIMMING BATH IS OPEN BETWEEN THE FOLLOWING HOURS

Gender	Charge	Time
GENTLEMEN	Free	6 a.m. to 9 a.m.
	1s 0d or 25 Cents.	2 p.m. to 7 p.m.
LADIES	Free	10 a.m. to noon.
	1s. 0d.	Noon to 1 p.m.

THE CHARGE INCLUDES USE OF COSTUME.

A GYMNASIUM fully supplied with modern appliances, is situated on the Boat Deck, and is open for exercise by Ladies and Gentlemen during the same hours as the Baths, no charge being made for the use of the appliances

The Gymnasium will be available for children from 1 to 3 p.m. only.

A SQUASH RACQUET COURT is provided on Deck F, and is in charge of a professional player. Tickets for the use of the Court may be obtained at the Enquiry Office at 2/– (or 50 cents) per half-hour, to include the services of the Professional if required. Balls may be purchased from the Professional, who is also authorised to sell and hire racquets.

The Court may be reserved in advance by application to the Professional in charge, and may not be occupied for longer than one hour at a time by the same players if others are waiting.

A CLOTHES PRESSING AND CLEANING ROOM is in charge of an expert attendant, who will carry out any work of this kind for Ladies and Gentlemen, in accordance with a fixed printed tariff of charges which can be had on application to the Bedroom Steward.

≈≈≈

FIRST CLASS
PASSENGER LIST
PER
ROYAL AND U.S. MAIL
S.S. "Titanic,"
FROM SOUTHAMPTON
& CHERBOURG
TO NEW YORK
(Via QUEENSTOWN).

Wednesday, 10th April,
1912.

≈≈≈

Allen, Miss Miss Elizabeth Walton
Allison, Mr. H. J.
Allison, Mrs. H. J. and Maid
Allison, Miss
Allison, Master and Nurse
Anderson, Mr. Harry
Andrews, Miss Cornelia I.
Andrews, Mr. Thomas
Appleton, Mrs. E. D.
Artagaveytia, Mr. Ramon
Astor, Colonel J. J. and Man
  servant
Astor, Mrs J. J. and Maid
Aubert, Mrs. N. and Maid

Barkworth, Mr. A. H.
Baumann, Mr. J.
Baxter, Mrs. James
Baxter, Mr. Quigg
Beattie, Mr. T.
Beckwith, Mr. R. L.
Beckwith, Mrs. R. L.
Behr, Mr. K. H.
Bishop, Mr. D. H.
Bishop, Mrs. D. H.
Bjornstrom, Mr. H.
Blackwell, Mr. Stephen Weart
Blank, Mr. Henry
Bonnell, Miss Caroline
Bonnell, Miss Lily

Borebank, Mr. J. J.
Bowen, Miss
Bowerman, Miss Elsie
Brady, Mr. John B.
Brandeis, Mr. E.
Brayton, Mr. George
Brewe, Dr. Arthur Jackson
Brown, Mrs. J. J.
Brown, Mrs. J. M.
Bucknell, Mrs. W. and Maid
Butt, Major Archibald W.

Calderhead, Mr. E. P.
Cardell, Mrs. Churchill
Cardeza, Mrs. J. W. M. and Maid
Cardeza, Mr. T. D. M. and Man
  servant
Carlson, Mr. Frank
Carran, Mr. J. P.
Carter, Mr. William E.
Carter, Mrs. William E. and Maid
Carter, Miss Lucile
Carter, Master William T.
Case, Mr. Howard B.
Cavendish, Mr. T. W.
Cavendish, Mrs. T. W. and Maid
Chaffee, Mr. Herbert F.
Chaffee, Mrs. Herbert F.
Chambers, Mr. N. C.
Chambers, Mrs. N. C.

Cherry, Miss Gladys
Chevré, Mr. Paul
Chibnall, Mrs. E. M. Bowerman
Chisholm, Mr. Robert
Clark, Mr. Walter M.
Clark, Mrs. Walter M.
Clifford, Mr. George Quincy
Colley, Mr. E. P.
Compton, Mrs. A. T.
Compton, Miss S. R.
Compton, Mr. A. T., Jr.
Cornell, Mrs. R C.
Crafton, Mr. John B.
Crosby, Mr. Edward G.
Crosby, Mrs. Edward G.
Crosby, Miss Harriet
Cummings, Mr. John Bradley
Cummings, Mrs. John Bradley

Daly, Mr. P. D.
Daniel, Mr. Robert W.
Davidson, Mr. Thornton
Davidson. Mrs. Thornton
de Villiers, Mrs. B.
Dick, Mr. A. A.
Dick, Mrs A. A.
Dodge, Mr. Washington
Dodge, Mrs. Washington
Dodge, Master Washington
Douglas, Mrs. F. C.

Douglas, Mr. W. D.
Douglas, Mrs. W. D. and Maid
Dulles, Mr. William C.

Earnshew, Mrs. Boulton
Endres, Miss Caroline
Eustis, Miss E. M.
Evans, Miss E.

Flegenheim, Mrs. A.
Flynn, Mr. J. I.
Foreman, Mr. B. L.
Fortune, Mr. Mark
Fortune, Mrs. Mark
Fortune, Miss Ethel
Fortune, Miss Alice
Fortune, Miss Mabel
Fortune, Mr Charles
Franklin, Mr. T. P.
Frauenthal, Mr. T. G.
Frauenthal, Dr. Henry W.
Frauenthal, Mrs Henry W.
Frolicher, Miss Marguerite
Futrelle, Mr. J.
Futrelle, Mrs. J.

Gee, Mr. Arthur
Gibson, Mrs. L.
Gibson, Miss D.
Goldenberg, Mr. E. L.
Goldenberg, Mrs. E. L.
Goldschmidt, Mr. George B.
Gracie, Colonel Archibald

Graham, Mr.
Graham, Mrs. William G.
Graham, Miss Margaret
Greenfield, Mrs. L. D.
Greenfield, Mr. W. B.
Giglio, Mr. Victor
Guggenheim, Mr. Benjamin

Harder, Mr. George A.
Harder, Mrs. George A.
Harper, Mr. Henry Sleeper and Manservant
Harper, Mrs. Henry Sleeper
Harris, Mr. Henry B.
Harris, Mrs. Henry B.
Harrison, Mr. W. H.
Haven, Mr. H.
Hawksford, Mr. W. J.
Hays, Mr. Charles M.
Hays, Mrs. Charles M. and Maid
Hays, Miss Margaret
Head, Mr. Christopher
Host, Mr. W. F.
Hilliard, Mr. Herbert Henry
Hipkins, Mr. W. E.
Hippach, Mrs. Ida S.
Hippach, Miss Jean
Hogeboom, Mrs. John C.
Holverson, Mr. A. O.
Holverson, Mrs. A. O.
Hoyt, Mr. Frederick M.
Hoyt, Mrs. Frederick M.

Isham, Miss A. E.
Ismay, Mr. and Manservant

Jakob, Mr. Birnbaum
Jones, Mr. C. C.
Julian, Mr. H. F.

Kent, Mr. Edward A.
Kenyon, Mr. F. R.
Kenyon, Mrs. F. R.
Kimball, Mr. E. N.
Kimball, Mrs. E. N.
Klaber, Mr. Herman

Lambert-Williams, Mr. Fletcher Fellowes
Leader, Mrs. F. A.
Levy, Mr. E. G.
Lines, Mrs. Ernest. H.
Lines, Miss Mary C.
Lindstroem, Mrs. J.
Long, Mr. Milton C.
Loring, Mr. J. H.
Longley, Miss Gretchem F.

Madill, Miss Georgette Alexandra
Maguire, Mr. J. E.
Marechal, Mr. Pierre
Marvin, Mr. D. W.
Marvin, Mrs. D. W.
McCaffry, Mr. T.
McCarthy, Mr. Timothy J.
McGough, Mr. J. R.

Melody, Mr. A.
Meyer, Mr. Edgar J.
Meyer, Mrs. Edgar J.
Millet, Mr. Frank D.
Minahan, Dr. W. E.
Minahan, Mrs. W. E.
Minahan, Miss Daisy
Molsom, Mr. H Markland
Moore, Mr. Clarence and Man servant
Morgan, Mr.
Morgan, Mrs. and Maid

Natsch, Mr. Charles
Newell, Mr. A. W.
Newell, Miss Alice
Newell, Miss Madeline
Newsom, Miss Helen
Nicholson, Mr. A. S.

Ostby, Mr. E. C.
Ostby, Miss Helen R.
Ovies, Mr. S.
Parr, Mr. M. H. W.
Partner, Mr. Austin
Payne, Mr. V.
Pears, Mr. Thomas
Pears, Mrs. Thomas
Penasco, Mr. Victor
Penasco, Mrs. Victor and Maid
Peuchen, Major Arthur
Porter, Mr. Walter Chamberlain
Potter, Mrs. Thomas, Jr.

Reuchlin, Mr. Jonkheer J. G.
Rheims, Mr. George
Robert, Mrs. Edward S. and Maid
Roebling, Mr. Washington A. 2nd
Rolmane, Mr. C.
Rood, Mr. Hugh R.
Rosenbaum, Miss
Ross, Mr. J. Hugo
Rothes, The Countess of and Maid
Rothschild, Mr. M.
Rothschild, Mrs. M.
Rowe, Mr. Alfred
Ryerson, Mr. Arthur
Ryerson, Mrs. Arthur and Maid
Ryerson, Miss
Ryerson, Miss
Ryerson, Master
Saalfeld, Mr. Adolphe
Saloman, Mr. A. L.
Schabert, Mr.
Seward, Mr. Frederic K.
Shutes, Miss E. W.
Silverthorne, Mr.
Silvey, Mr. William B.
Silvey, Mrs. William B.
Simonius, Mr. Oberst Alfons
Sloper, Mr. William T.
Smart, Mr. John M.
Smith, Mr. J Clinch

Smith, Mr. R. W.
Snyder, Mr. John
Snyder, Mrs. John
Spedden, Mr. Frederick O.
Spedden, Mrs. Frederick O. and Maid
Spedden, Master R. Douglas and Nurse
Spencer, Mr. W. A.
Spencer, Mrs. W. A. and Maid
Stahelin, Dr. Max
Stead, Mr. W. T.
Stehli, Mr. Max Frolicher
Stehli, Mrs. Max Frolicher
Stengel, Mr. C. E. H.
Stengel, Mrs. C. E. H.
Stephenson, Mrs. W. B.
Stewart, Mr. A. A.
Stone, Mrs. George M. and Maid
Straus, Mr. Isidor and Manservant
Straus, Mrs. Isidor and Maid
Sutton, Mr. Frederick
Swift, Mrs. Frederick Joel
Taussig, Mr. Emil
Taussig, Mrs. Emil
Taussig, Miss Ruth
Taylor, Mr. E. Z.
Taylor, Mrs. E. Z.
Thayer, Mr. J. B.
Thayer, Mrs. J. B. and Maid
Thayer, Mr. J. B., Jr.

Thorne, Mr. G.
Thorne, Mrs. G.
Tucker, Mr. G. M., Jr.

Uruchurtu. Mr. M. R.

Van der Hoef, Mr. Wyckoff

Walker, Mr. W. Anderson
Warren, Mr. F. M.
Warren, Mrs. F. M.
Weir, Mr. J
White, Mr. M. J.
White, Mr. Percival W.
White, Mr. Richard F.
White, Mrs. J Stuart Maid, and Manservant
Wick, Mr. George D.
Wick, Mrs George D.
Wick, Miss Mary
Widener, Mr. George D. and Manservant
Widener, Mrs. George D. and Maid
Widener, Mr. Harry
Willard, Miss Constance
Williams, Mr. Duane
Williams, Mr. R. M. Jr.
Woolner, Mr. Hugh
Wright, Mr. George
Young, Miss Marie

R.M.S. "TITANIC"

BREAKFAST.

BAKED APPLES   FRESH FRUIT   STEWED PRUNES
QUAKER OATS BOILED HOMINY   PUFFED RICE
FRESH HERRINGS
FINDON HADDOCK   SMOKED SALMON
GRILLED MUTTON KIDNEYS & BACON
GRILLED HAM   GRILLED SAUSAGE
LAMB COLLOPS   VEGETABLE STEW
FRIED, SHIRRED, POACHED & BOILED EGGS
PLAIN & TOMATO OMELETTES TO ORDER
SIRLOIN STEAK & MUTTON CHOPS TO ORDER
MASHED, SAUTÉ & JACKET POTATOES
COLD MEAT
VIENNA & GRAHAM ROLLS
SODA & SULTANA SCONES   CORN BREAD
BUCKWHEAT CAKES
BLACK CURRANT CONSERVE   NARBONNE HONEY
OXFORD MARMALADE
WATERCRESS

R.M.S. "TITANIC"

LUNCHEON

CONSOMMÉ FERMIER   COCKIE LEEKIE

EGG   A   L'ARGENTEUIL

CHICKEN   A   LA   MARYLAND

CORNED BEEF,   VEGETABLES,   DUMPLINGS

FROM THE GRILL

GRILLED   MUTTON   CHOPS

MASHED, FRIED & BAKED JACKET POTATOES

CUSTARD PUDDING

APPLE MERINGUE   PASTRY

BUFFET

SALMON MAYONNAISE   POTTED SHRIMPS

NORWEGIAN ANCHOVIES   SOUSED HERRINGS

PLAIN & SMOKED SARDINES

ROAST BEEF

ROUND   OF   SPICED BEEF

VEAL & HAM PIE

VIRGINIA & CUMBERLAND HAM

BOLOGNA SAUSAGE   BRAWN

GALANTINE OF CHICKEN

CORNED OX TONGUE

LETTUCE   BEETROOT   TOMATOES

CHEESE

CHESHIRE, STILTON, GORGONZOLA,   EDAM,

CAMEMBERT, ROQUEFORT, ST. IVEL.

CHEDDAR

Iced draught Munich Lager Beer 3d. & 6d. a Tankard

R.M.S. "TITANIC"

FIRST CLASS DINNER.

HORS D'OEUVRE VARIÈS

OYSTERS

CONSOMME OLGA   CREAM OF BARLEY

SALMON, MOUSSELINE SAUCE, CUCUMBER

FILET MIGNONS LILI

SAUTÉ OF CHICKEN LYONNAISE

VEGETABLE MARROW FARCIE

LAMB, MINT SAUCE

ROAST DUCKLING, APPLE SAUCE

SIRLOIN OF BEEF   CHATEAU POTATOES

GREEN PEAS   CREAMED CARROTS

BOILED RICE

PARMENTIER & BOILED NEW POTATOES

PUNCH ROMAINE

ROAST SQUAB & CRESS

RED BURGUNDY

COLD ASPARAGUS   VINAIGRETTE

PÂTÉ DE FOIE GRAS

CELERY

WALDORF PUDDING

PEACHES EN CHARTREUSE JELLY

CHOCOLATE & VANILLA ECLAIRS

FRENCH ICE CREAM

GENERAL INFORMATION FOR PASSENGERS IN THE SECOND CLASS

ALL RATES QUOTED ARE SUBJECT TO CHANGE WITHOUT NOTICE

CONDITIONS OF TRANSPORTATION.—The attention of passengers is specially directed to the conditions of transportation as set forth on the steamer contract ticket.

ROUND TRIP.—The round trip rate consists of the combined East and West-bound fares according to steamer and accommodations without any deduction.

INTERCHANGEABLE RETURN TICKETS.—Trans-Atlantic Passengers travelling by the White Star Line and purchasing Round Trip Tickets will have the privilege of using the return portion of their tickets by either the White Star Line or by the American Line, Atlantic Transport, Dominion Leyland, Red Star or White Star-Dominion Lines from any of their Trans-Atlantic Ports. The return ticket will also be available by the Cunard, French, Hamburg-American, Holland-America, North German Lloyd or Austro-Americana Lines, and passengers holding return tickets issued by any of these lines may return by the White Star Line. The return ticket to be subject to the rules and regulations of the line by which the passenger desires to return.

SURGEON.—Each steamer carries an experienced Surgeon who is authorized to make customary charges, subject in each Case to the approval of the Commander, for treating passengers at their request for any illness not originating on board the ship. In the case of sickness developed on board, no charge will be made, and medicine will be provided free in all circumstances.

STEWARDESSES are also carried to attend ladies and children.

RESERVATION OF BERTHS.—Berths can be secured in advance on payment of **$10.00** per adult. Berths for the return voyage also, can be secured when engaging the outward passage. When return accommodation is secured in advance, the actual contract ticket must be issued in all instances, or the reservation will not hold good.

BAGGAGE.—Each adult Second Class passenger is allowed twenty cubic feet of baggage free, excess will be charged at the rate of 25 cents per cubic foot. Packages required on the voyage should not exceed 14 inches in height,

2 feet in width and 3 feet in length. All large pieces must go in the hold. Tags furnished on applications. Passengers intending to land at Plymouth, Cherbourg, or Queenstown, should have their baggage labelled accordingly. Merchandise, house furniture, pianos etc., are not considered baggage and will be charged as freight according to agreement. Baggage must be claimed on pier before embarking, otherwise it may remain there at passenger's risk.

BICYCLES must be crated and will be carried only at owner's risk. The charge from the port of embarkation to the port of debarkation is $2.50 each.

DECK CHAIRS AND RUGS can be hired at a charge of $1.00 each—12 hours notice should be given.

DOGS, CATS, MONKEYS.—The charge for Dogs is **$10.00** each. Rates for Cats and Monkeys on application. Birds, etc., **$2.50** for each cage. These charges do not include the customary Butcher's fee. Dogs, Cats and Monkeys must be caged before being brought upon the steamer and will then be placed in charge of the Butcher. Dogs to be landed in England require special license from the Secretary of the Board of Agriculture in London. Without such permit they will not be received on board ship. Particulars on application.

VALUABLES.—The White Star Line has provided a safe in the office of the Purser, in which passengers may deposit money, jewels or ornaments, for safe keeping. The Company will not be liable to passengers for the loss of money, jewels or ornaments, by theft or otherwise not so deposited.

ADDITIONAL PASSAGE MONEY OR FREIGHT, when paid on board, should be receipted for on the Company's forms.

BAGGAGE INSURANCE

The Company's liability for baggage is strictly limited, but arrangements have been made where passengers can have their baggage and personal effects insured anywhere in the world from the time it leaves home against loss or damage by fire or lightning, and practically all risks and perils of transportation and navigation on land or water.

This insurance is issued in the form of Tourists' Baggage Tickets by the St. Paul Fire and Marine Insurance Company of St. Paul, Minn. For sale by our Agents and at our own offices. Cost per week, 25 cents per $150. Maximum amount each person $6,000.

The White Star Line strongly recommends that passengers insure their baggage whenever practicable, as in the event of loss or damage to baggage, the Company cannot under any circumstances accept any liability beyond the amount specified on the steamer contract ticket.

— **Apply at any agency or office of the White Star Line.**

LANDING.— Second Class passengers are landed in New York at the White Star Line Pier the same as the First Class passengers.

BAGGAGE CHECKED from pier at New York to destination. Upon landing at New York, and on application to the uniformed representatives of the Railroads who meet all arriving White Star Line steamers, Railroad Tickets may be purchased, and baggage of First and Second Class passengers may be checked from the Steamship Pier to any point along the lines of the Principal Railroads.

QUEENSTOWN DEPARTURES.— Second Class passengers joining the White Star Mail Steamers from Southampton at Queenstown, and paying less than $50 must be at that port not later than eight o'clock on the Thursday morning. Those paying $50 or over, may embark with the First Class passengers, and must be at Queenstown not later than 10.15 o'clock on the Thursday morning. Second Class passengers joining the steamers of the Liverpool New York Service at Queenstown, must be at that port not later than the evening of the day of the steamers departure from Liverpool.

TRAVELERS CHECKS.— These checks are issued at the principal offices and agencies of this Company in America and are available all over the world. Each check shows upon its face the exact amount which will be paid in foreign money in the different countries in Europe. Tourists will find these checks the most convenient form in which to carry their funds. The advantage of being able to arrange with the same Company for both passage and traveling funds will also be appreciated by our patrons. Further information on application.

BUY OUR INTERNATIONAL TRAVELERS CHECKS

SAFE——WIDELY AVAILABLE——CONVENIENT

WHITE STAR LINE

MAIL AND PASSENGER STEAMERS

WHITE STAR-DOMINION CANADIAN SERVICE

(ROYAL MAIL STEAMERS)

Second Class Rates, 1912

OLYMPIC

45,324 Tons

The
World's Largest
and Finest
Steamers

TITANIC

45,000 Tons

The
World's Largest
and Finest
Steamers

NEW YORK - CHERBOURG - SOUTHAMPTON
(Via Plymouth Eastbound and via Queenstown Westbound)

NEW YORK - QUEENSTOWN - LIVERPOOL

BOSTON - QUEENSTOWN - LIVERPOOL

MONTREAL - QUEBEC - LIVERPOOL

PORTLAND - LIVERPOOL

OFFICES:
9 BROADWAY, NEW YORK
Pier 62 North River (Foot of West 23rd Street), New York

84 STATE STREET, BOSTON   **118 NOTRE DAME STREET W., MONTREAL**

CHICAGO............Cor. Washington & La Salle Sts.	QUEBEC......................53 Dalhousie Street
HALIFAX, N. S......................159 Hollis Street	SAN FRANCISCO..................319 Geary Street
MINNEAPOLIS..............121 South Third Street	SEATTLE......................619 Second Avenue
NEW ORLEANS............219 St. Charles Street	ST. LOUIS......................900 Locust Street
PHILADELPHIA..............1319 Walnut Street	TORONTO................41 King Street, East
PORTLAND, ME.....................1 India Street	WASHINGTON..............1306 F Street, N. W
	WINNIPEG, 338 Main St., S. E. Cor. Portage Ave.

No. 1.

New York, January, 1912   J-20 C1029

On every occasion when referring to berths, please mention Deck Initial as well as Stateroom Number

SECOND CLASS ☆ OCEAN RATES

Available only for Tickets Purchased in America

FROM NEW YORK TO PLYMOUTH - CHERBOURG♦ - SOUTHAMPTON   FROM SOUTHAMPTON - CHERBOURG♦ - QUEENSTOWN TO NEW YORK

The Company reserves the right to alter Passage Rates without notice.   Return Tickets issued on payment of the combined Eastbound and Westbound fares.

THE WORLD'S LARGEST AND FINEST STEAMERS

U. S. & R. M. S. "OLYMPIC" 45,324 TONS and "TITANIC" 45,000 TONS

RAILROAD FARES
From PLYMOUTH to LONDON, 3rd Class, $3.75
Between SOUTHAMPTON and LONDON,
2nd Class, $1.75   3rd Class, $1.40
Between CHERBOURG and PARIS
2nd Class, $6.   3rd Class, $3.00

	WINTER SEASON — NEW YORK to PLYMOUTH or SOUTHAMPTON before May 1 and after July 15. SOUTHAMPTON/QUEENSTOWN to NEW YORK before August 15 and after September 30 PER ADULT	SUMMER SEASON (Eastbound) From NEW YORK May 1 to July 15 To PLYMOUTH or SOUTHAMPTON					SUMMER SEASON (Westbound) From SOUTHAMPTON or QUEENSTOWN August 15 to September 30				
		For 4 Adults each	For 3½	For 3 ADULTS IN A ROOM Per Room	For 2½ In a Room	For 2	For 4 Adults each	For 3½	For 3 ADULTS IN A ROOM Per Room	For 2½ In a Room	For 2
SALOON DECK "D"—"Olympic" and "Titanic"											
Outside Rooms	67.50	$72.50	$277.50	$265.00	$262.50	$240	$77.50	$297.50	$285	$272.50	$260
	67.50	70.00	267.50	255.00	252.50	230	75.00	287.50	275	262.50	250 / 180
	68.00	67.50	257.50	245.00	242.50	180	72.50	277.50	265	252.50	240
Inside Rooms	68.00	70.00	267.50	255.00	252.50	230	75.00	287.50	275	262.50	170 / 176
	65.00	67.50	257.50	245.00	242.50	180	72.50	277.50	265	252.50	
	65.00	65.00	247.50	235.00	232.50	155	70.00	267.50	255	242.50	
MAIN DECK "E"—"Olympic" and "Titanic"											
Outside Rooms	66.00	70.00	267.50	255.00	242.50	230	75.00	287.50	276	262.50	250
	66.00 / 64.00	67.50	257.50	245.00	232.50	220 / 180	72.50	277.50	265	252.50	240 / 170
	65.00	65.00	247.50	235.00	222.50	210	70.00	267.50	255	242.50	230
Inside Rooms	65.00	65.00				145					165
	65.00	65.00				140					160
MIDDLE DECK "F"—"Olympic" and "Titanic"											
Outside Rooms	67.50	70.00	267.50	255.00	242.50	220	75.00	287.50	275	262.50	250
	65.00	67.50	257.50	245.00	232.50	210 / 145	72.50	277.50	265	252.50	240 / 170
	65.00	65.00	247.50	235.00	222.50	210	70.00	267.50	255	242.50	230
Inside Rooms	65.00	65.00				140					165 / 168
	65.00	65.00				180					160
ROOMS NOT INCLUDED IN THE ABOVE	65.00	65.00				180	70.00 and up				145 and up

SALOON DECK "D"—"Olympic" and "Titanic"

Outside Rooms
{ 4 Berths.—D53, D54, D57, D58, D65, D66, D71.
{ 2 Berths.—D59, D60, D67, D68, D73, D74, D87.
{ 2 Berths.—D85*, D86†

Inside Rooms
{ 4 Berths.—D76, D80
{ 2 Berths.—D31†, D55†, D56†, D61†, D62†.
{ 2 Berths.—D63†, D75†, D79†, D89†.
{ 2 Berths.—D69†, D70†, D77†, D78†, D81†, D82†

MAIN DECK "E"—"Olympic" and "Titanic"

"OLYMPIC"   "TITANIC"

Outside Rooms
{ 4 Berths.—E89,   4 Berths.—E89, E98.
  E92, E95, E99,   E90, E100, E103,
  E104, E96, E100,   E92, E95, E101, E104.
  E104.
{ 2 Berths.—E103,   2 Berths.—E99,
  E107.   E106
{ 2 Berths.—E105   2 Berths.—E92†, E96†,
  E104   E94.

Inside Rooms
{ 2 Berths.—E96,   2 Berths.—E99.
  E98†, E91†.   E98†
{ 2 Berths.—E87†, E98.   2 Berths.—E91, E102.
  E101   E105.

MIDDLE DECK "F"—"Olympic" and "Titanic"

Outside Rooms
{ 4 Berths.—F25, E90, F10, F19, F26, F28, F38, F88.
{ 4 Berths.—F8, F4, F7, F78, F11, F12, F21, F27.
{ 4 Berths.—F53, F57, F61, F92, F57, F45, F52.
{ 2 Berths.—F18, F22, F64, F56, F64, F69

Inside Rooms
{ 2 Berths.—F31, F33, F39, F42, F51, F55, F63.
{ 2 Berths.—F24†, F32†, F33†, F38†, F41†, F45†, F47†.
  F50, F55.

ROOMS NOT INCLUDED IN THE ABOVE

* Sofa in Room sufficiently large to accommodate one child.   The size of each Sofa is indicated on the plan.

† Sofa in Room sufficiently large to accommodate one child.

Triple Screw Steamer "TITANIC."

_____

2ND. CLASS

APRIL 14, 1912.

BREAKFAST.

ROLLED OATS   BOILED HOMINY

FRESH FISH   YARMOUTH BLOATERS

GRILLED OX KIDNEYS & BACON

AMERICAN DRY HASH AU GRATIN

GRILLED SAUSAGE   MASHED POTATOES

GRILLED HAM & FRIED EGGS

FRIED POTATOES

VIENNA & GRAHAM ROLLS   SODA SCONES

BUCKWHEAT CAKES

MAPLE SYRUP CONSERVE

MARMALADE

TEA   COFFEE

WATERCRESS

TRIPLE SCREW STEAMER "TITANIC."

2ND. CLASS

APRIL 14, 1912.

LUNCHEON.

PEA SOUP

SPAGHETTI   AU   GRATIN

CORNED BEEF VEGETABLE DUMPLINGS

ROAST MUTTON

BAKED JACKET POTATOES

COLD   ROAST MUTTON

ROAST BEEF   SAUSAGE OX TONGUE

PICKLES   SALAD   TAPIOCA

PUDDING   APPLE TART

FRESH FRUIT   CHEESE   BISCUITS

COFFEE

TRIPLE SCREW STEAMER "TITANIC."

2ND. CLASS

APRIL 14, 1912.

DINNER.

CONSOMMÉ TAPIOCA

BAKED HADDOCK,   SHARP SAUCE

CURRIED CHICKEN & RICE

SPRING LAMB, MINT SAUCE

ROAST TURKEY, CRANBERRY SAUCE

GREEN PEAS   PURÉE TURNIPS

BOILED RICE   BOILED & ROAST POTATOES

PLUM PUDDING   WINE JELLY

COCOANUT SANDWICH

AMERICAN ICE CREAM   NUTS ASSORTED

FRESH FRUIT   CHEESE & BISCUITS

COFFEE

WHITE STAR LINE
Specimen Third Class Bill of Fare
Subject to Alteration as Circumstances Require

	Sunday	Monday	Tuesday	Wednesday	Thursday	Friday	Saturday
Breakfast	Quaker Oats and Milk	Oatmeal Porridge and Milk	Oatmeal Porridge and Milk	Quaker Oats and Milk	Oatmeal Porridge and Milk	Quaker Oats and Milk	Oatmeal Porridge and Milk
	Smoked Herrings and Jacket Potatoes	Irish Stew	Ling Fish, Egg Sauce	Smoked Herrings	Liver and Bacon	Smoked Herrings	Vegetable Stew
	Boiled Eggs	Broiled Sausages	Fried Tripe and Onions	Beefsteak and Onions	Irish Stew	Jacket Potatoes	Fried Tripe and Onions
	Fresh Bread and Butter	Fresh Bread and Butter	Jacket Potatoes	Jacket Potatoes	Fresh Bread and Butter	Curried Beef and Rice	Fresh Bread and Butter
	Marmalade, Swedish Bread	Marmalade, Swedish Bread	Fresh Bread and Butter	Fresh Bread and Butter	Marmalade, Swedish Bread	Fresh Bread and Butter	Marmalade, Swedish Bread
	Tea and Coffee	Tea and Coffee	Marmalade, Swedish Bread	Marmalade, Swedish Bread	Tea and Coffee	Marmalade, Swedish Bread	Tea and Coffee
			Tea and Coffee	Tea and Coffee		Tea and Coffee	
Dinner	Vegetable Soup	Barley Broth	Pea Soup	Rice Soup	Vegetable Soup	Pea Soup	Bouillon Soup
	Roast Pork, Sage and Onions	Beefsteak and Kidney Pie	Fricasse Rabbit and Bacon	Corned Beef and Cabbage	Boiled Mutton and Caper Sauce	Ling Fish, Egg Salad	Roast Beef and Brown Gravy
	Green Peas	Carrots and Turnips	Lima Beans, Boiled Potatoes	Boiled Potatoes	Green Peas, Boiled Potatoes	Cold Beef and Pickles	Green Beans, Boiled Potatoes
	Boiled Potatoes	Boiled Potatoes	Cabin Biscuits, Fresh Bread	Cabin Biscuits, Fresh Bread	Cabin Biscuits, Fresh Bread	Cabbage, Boiled Potatoes	Cabin Biscuits, Fresh Bread
	Cabin Biscuits, Fresh Bread	Cabin Biscuits, Fresh Bread	Semolina Pudding	Peaches and Rice	Plum Pudding, Sweet Sauce	Cabin Biscuits, Fresh Bread	Prunes and Rice
	Plum Pudding, Sweet Sauce	Stewed Apples and Rice	Apples			Cerealine Pudding	
	Oranges					Oranges	
Tea	Ragout of Beef, Potatoes and Pickles	Curried Mutton and Rice	Haricot Mutton	Brawn	Sausage and Mashed Potatoes	Cod Fish Cakes	Rabbit Pie
	Apricots	Cheese and Pickles	Pickles	Cheese and Pickles	Dry Hash	Cheese and Pickles	Baked Potatoes
	Fresh Bread and Butter	Fresh Bread and Butter	Prunes and Rice	Fresh Bread and Butter	Apples and Rice	Fresh Bread and Butter	Fresh Bread and Butter
	Currant Buns	Damson Jam	Fresh Bread and Butter	Rhubarb Jam	Fresh Bread and Butter	Plum and Apple Jam	Rhubarb and Ginger Jam
	Tea	Swedish Bread	Swedish Bread	Currant Buns	Swedish Bread	Swedish Bread	Swedish Bread
		Tea	Tea	Tea	Tea	Tea	Tea

SUPPER—Every Day.—Cabin Biscuits and Cheese. Gruel, Coffee.

Fresh Fish served as substitute for Salt Fish as opportunity offers

Kosher Meat Supplied and Cooked for Jewish Passengers as desired.

Any complaint regarding the Food supplied, want of attention or incivility, should be at once reported to the Purser or Chief-Steward. For purposes of identification, each Steward wears a numbered badge on the arm.

Part Four
OPERATION, SAFETY
& NAVIGATION

Captain E. J. Smith, R.D. (Commr. R.N.R.).

~Ship's Officers~

Captain, E. J. Smith, R.D. (Commr. R.N.R.) ~ *Captain*
Lt. Henry Tingle Wilde, R.N.R ~ *Chief Officer*
Lt. William McMaster Murdoch, R.N.R ~ *First Officer*
Sub-Lt. Charles Herbert Lightoller, R.N.R ~ *Second Officer*
Mr Herbert John Pitman ~ *Third Officer*
Sub-Lt. Joseph Groves Boxhall, R.N.R ~ *Fourth Officer*
Sub-Lt. Harold Godfrey Lowe, R.N.R ~ *Fifth Officer*
Mr. Paul James Moody ~ *Sixth Officer*

~Complement~

Mr. W. F. N. O'Loughlin ~ *Surgeon*
Mr. J. E. Simpson ~ *Asst. Surgeon*
Mr. H. W. McElroy ~ *Purser*
Mr. R. L. Barker ~ *Asst. Purser*
Mr. A. A. Ashcroft ~ *Clerk*
Mr. E. W. King ~ *Clerk*
Mr. J. R. Rice ~ *Clerk*
Mr. D. S. Campbell ~ *Third Class Clerk*
Mr. J. G. Phillips ~ *Telegraphist*
Mr. H. S. Bride ~ *Asst. Telegraphist*
Mr. A. L. Latimer ~ *Chief Steward*
Mr. J. T. Hardy ~ *Chief Second Class Steward*
Mr. J. W. Kieran ~ *Chief Third Class Steward*
Mr. J. A. Paintin ~ *Captain's Steward*
Mr. T. W. McCawley ~ *Gymnasium Steward*
Mr. F. Wright ~ *Squash Court Steward*

NORTH ATLANTIC LANE ROUTES

As agreed to by the principal Steamship Companies, take effect from January 15th, 1899, and now issued general information.

WESTBOUND.

FROM 15th JANUARY TO 14th AUGUST, BOTH DAYS INCLUSIVE

Steer from Fastnet, or Bishop Rock, on GREAT CIRCLE course, but nothing South, to cross the meridian of 47° West in Latitude 42° North, thence by either rhumb line, or Great Circle (or even North of the Great Circle, if an easterly current is encountered), to a position South of Nantucket Light-Vessel, thence to Fire Island Light-Vessel, when bound for New York, or to Five Fathom Bank South Light-Vessel, when bound for Philadelphia.

FROM 15th AUGUST TO 14th JANUARY, BOTH DAYS INCLUSIVE.

Steer from Fastnet, or Bishop Rock, on GREAT CIRCLE course, but nothing South, to cross the meridian of 49° West in Latitude 46° North, thence by rhumb line, to cross the meridian of 60° West in Latitude 46° North, thence also by rhumb line, to a position South of Nantucket Light-Vessel, thence to Fire Island Light-Vessel, when bound for New York, or to Five Fathom Bank South Light-Vessel, when bound for Philadelphia.

EASTBOUND.

At all seasons of the year, steer a course from Sandy Hook Light-Vessel, or Five Fathom Bank South Light-Vessel, to cross the meridian of 70° West, nothing to the northward of Lat. 40° 10'.

FROM 15th JANUARY TO 23rd AUGUST, BOTH DAYS INCLUSIVE.

Steer from 40° 10' North, and 70° West, by rhumb line, to cross the meridian of 47° West in Latitude 41° North, and from this last position nothing North of the GREAT CIRCLE to Fastnet, when bound to the Irish Channel, or nothing North of the GREAT CIRCLE to Bishop Rock, when bound to the English Channel.

FROM 24th AUGUST TO 14th JANUARY, BOTH DAYS INCLUSIVE.

Steer from Latitude 40° 10' North, and Longitude 70° West, to cross the meridian of 60° West in Latitude 42° 0' North, thence by rhumb line to cross the meridian of 45° West in Latitude 46° 30' North, and from this last position nothing North of the GREAT CIRCLE to Fastnet, when bound to the Irish Channel, and as near as possible to, but nothing North of the GREAT CIRCLE to Bishop Rock, always keeping South of the Latitude of Bishop Rock, when bound to the English Channel.

GENERAL INSTRUCTION.

When courses are changed at the intersections of meridians any time before or after noon, you will note in your logs both distances to and from the meridians, that the ship has sailed from noon to noon, and not the distance from the position at noon the day before to the position at noon the day after the meridian is crossed.

White Star Line United States & Royal Mail Steamers

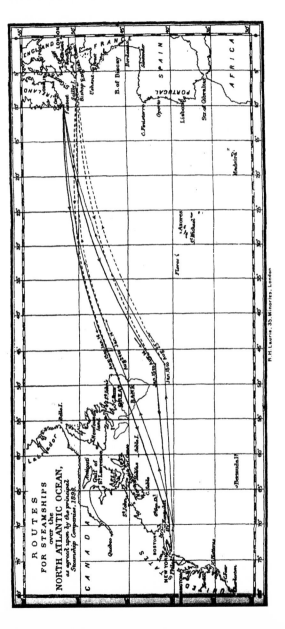

Working Arrangements of the Ships

The working arrangements on board the *Olympic* and *Titanic* are necessarily on a scale in keeping with the great size of the vessels. The number of crew employed on board each ship for all purposes is about 860. Of these about 65 belong to the navigating department, 320 are employed in the engineers' department, and 475 are engaged in the stewards' and catering department. The forward portion of the boat deck and the exposed decks at the ends of the vessel are entirely devoted to working and navigating appliances, while the management of the ship is also greatly facilitated by the working passage on the port side of E deck, which extends nearly the full length of this deck and is connected by stairways with all the principal departments.

Accommodation for Officers and Crew

The position of the officers' and crews' accommodation will be seen from the general arrangements of the ship. The officers are accommodated in a house on the boat deck forward. The engineers' quarters are on the middle deck, and their mess room, pantries, offices, etc., on the deck above adjoining the working passage. The firemen have excellent accommodation on five decks right forward. Access from their quarters to the boiler rooms is obtained by two spiral staircases and a tunnel through the forward holds, an arrangement which keeps the firemen entirely clear of the passenger accommodation. The seamen's accommodation is placed on E deck forward. The living rooms for the stewards and catering staff are situated on the port side of E deck, and are entered from the working passage.

Cargo, Baggage and Mails

To provide access for cargo or baggage to the lower holds, three cargo hatchways, placed at the centre-line of the ship, have been fitted forward for Nos. 1, 2 and 3 holds; four hatchways have been provided aft, two placed at the centre-line for Nos. 5 and 6 holds; and two smaller hatchways, away from the centre-line, give access to No. 4 hold. The hatch ways to Nos. 1 and 2 holds are served by three steam winches. The third hatch, that near the passengers' quarters, is served by two 2-ton electric cranes and two 3-ton electric winches. The two hatchways to No.4 hold are each served by a 1-ton electric crane. The remaining hatch-ways,

Nos. 5 and 6, are each served by two 2-ton cranes and one 3-ton electric winch. The masts, which have a height of 205ft. above the average draught line, are utilized for working the cargo by means of cargo spans, while the foremast supports a derrick suitable for lifting motor cars, which will be stored in one of the fore holds. The post office and baggage accommodation is arranged compactly on the lower and orlop decks forward, with a view to expediting the reception and despatch of the mails and the transportation of passengers' baggage on the departure and arrival of the ship.

The Navigating Bridge

The navigating bridge, from which the vessel is controlled, is situated at the forward end of the boat deck, so that the navigating officer may have a clear view ahead. This bridge is a veritable forest of instruments. In the centre is the wheel house, containing the telemotor control wheel by which the ship is steered, with a standard compass immediately in front. In front of the wheel house are placed the engine room, docking, and steering telegraphs, and loud-speaking telephones to various stations. In the bridge shelter or chart room adjoining are also placed the watertight door controller, the submarine-signal receiver, the helm indicator, the master clocks, and other apparatus. There is also a docking bridge provided right aft, for use when the vessel is docking or turning in a confined space.

Navigating Appliances

The navigating appliances are most complete. In addition to the two compasses on the captain's bridge and one on the docking bridge aft, there is a standard compass on an isolated brass-work platform in the centre of the ship, at a height of 12 feet above all iron-work and 78 feet above the water-line. Adjacent to the bridge there are two electrically-driven sounding machines, arranged with spars to enable soundings to be taken when the ship is going at a good speed. All observations can thus be taken under the direct control of the officer in command. The telegraphs are by Messrs. J. W. Ray & Co., of Liverpool, and communicate with engine-room, capstan and other stations. As already indicated, there is also telemotor gear for the steering of the ship. The vessels are fitted with complete installation for receiving submarine signals.

Mooring and Warping Arrangements

Special attention has been devoted by the builders to the mooring arrangements of the new vessels. It was realized that a size of ship had been reached for which the usual arrangement of two bower anchors was insufficient, and it was decided to have, in addition to these, a centre anchor worked by a wire rope through the extra hawsepipe in the stem, to which reference has already been made. The centre anchor weighs $15\frac{1}{2}$ tons, and the side anchors each weigh $7\frac{3}{4}$ tons. The cables used in connection with the side anchors are 3in. diameter and have a total length of 330 fathoms, weighing in all 96 tons. The anchors are of Hall's latest improved type, and, with the cables, have been manufactured by Messrs. N. Hingley & Sons, Ltd., of Netherton, Dudley. A strongly built crane is fitted at the centre-line of the forecastle deck for handling the 15 ton anchor, which is placed in a well on the deck immediately abaft the stem. The side anchors are housed in the hawsepipes in the usual manner.

The wire hawser used in connection with the centre anchor is $9\frac{1}{2}$ in. circumference and 175 fathoms long, and has been supplied, in the case of both the *Olympic* and *Titanic*, by Messrs. Bullivant and Co., Ltd., of London. These hawsers, together with the thimbles and splices necessary,

The $15\frac{1}{2}$ ton anchor.

were guaranteed by the makers to withstand a breaking strain of 280 tons. At the request of the Board of Trade, one thimble and splice were tested to destruction at Cardiff in the presence of their surveyor, with the result that the test specimen broke near the tail of the splice at a load of 289 tons.

The introduction of the centre anchor has necessitated an addition to the usual Napier windlass gear in the form of a large grooved drum for winding the $9\frac{1}{2}$-in. hawser mentioned above. This drum, which is placed on the shelter deck right forward, is driven through worm gear by one of the windlass engines. The windlass drums, or cable holders, for winding the cables are placed on the forecastle deck. Each drum is mounted upon a vertical spindle, which is carried down to the shelter deck. Upon the lower end of each spindle is keyed a bevel wheel of large diameter, which is driven by worm gearing from one of the vertical windlass engines situated under the forecastle. Clutch-engaging and brake gear has been fitted and every detail embodied to ensure the satisfactory working of the cables under all conditions.

Ample arrangements have been made for warping the vessel in harbour. The forward gear for this purpose consists of four capstan drums placed on the forecastle, and one at a lower level for handling smaller ropes. The two foremost capstan spindles are driven by worm and bevel gearing in a similar manner to that adopted in the case of the windlass drums. The same engines are arranged to perform either of the set duties, a system of clutches enabling the windlass drum to be thrown out of gear while the engine is working the capstan drums, and vice versa. The second pair of capstan drums are driven independently by vertical engines placed on the shelter deck beneath them. Similar warping capstans are installed at the after end of the ship. At this end there are five drums with four steam engines, one of which actuates two capstans. For securing wire hawsers and warps, a large number of mooring bollards have been provided. These bollards are of very large size.

Boats & Davits

The lifeboats, which are 30ft. long, are placed on the boat deck. The davits are of the Welin double-acting type manufactured by the Welin Davit and Engineering Co., Ltd., of London. Sixteen sets, specially designed for handling two or, if desired, three boats each, have been provided. The double-acting system is not altogether new, as it was adopted by another company some time ago in the case of boats carried on the poop, but its employment on such a large scale is a distinct departure. The well-known principle of the Welin davit is retained in all its simplicity, with the addition of a slight segmental increase at the inboard edge of the quadrant. This modification enables the arm to be swung right inboard so that it may plumb the inboard boat, and thereby save the time-wasting operation of shoving and pulling the latter into position, which has to be done with davits of the ordinary type.

The arrangement for saving fore and aft deck space is also worthy of notice. Instead of having two separate standards between each boat, the standards are combined in the form of a twin frame. The latter carries the two quadrants and all the necessary gear for operating the forward and after boat at will. The operating gear is also of an ingenious and interesting nature. For this purpose a swing handle is employed, driving a small pinion, which is mounted upon a swing bar. The latter is thrown into or out of gear by means of a simple eccentric arrangement, which enables either screw of either davit to be worked independently of the other. For hoisting and lowering the boats, four 15-cwt. electric winches have been provided.

Compasses

The compass outfit consists of four of Lord Kelvin's latest patent standard compasses, supplied by Messrs. Kelvin and James White, Ltd. Two of these compasses are placed on the captain's bridge, one on the docking bridge aft, and one on an isolated brass work platform in the centre of the ship, which is built up from the boat deck 12ft. above all ironwork and 78ft. above the water-line.

Sounding Machines

Adjacent to the navigating bridge are two of Lord Kelvin's patent motor-driven sounding machines, arranged with spars to enable soundings to be taken when the ship is going at a good speed. The design of the machines is well known, but the latest pattern embodies an improvement in the form of an illuminated dial for night use. The illumination is provided by an electric lamp fitted on the top of the machine. The arrangement is such that the dial rotates, and only the figures adjacent to a pointer on the lamp case are illuminated.

Submarine Signalling

Both the *Olympic* and *Titanic* have been fitted with the Submarine Signal Co.'s apparatus for receiving submarine signals. With this system the sound of submarine bells is received through the hull of the vessel. By locating the direction of the sounds, the position of the vessel, when in the neighbourhood of the coast, can be accurately ascertained. The bells are established by the Trinity House and the lighting authorities of the United States, and over 120 are now in operation. The system is a great improvement upon that of aerial fog signals, as the latter, owing to the variations in the density of the atmosphere, are frequently misleading; and water, being constant in density, allows the sound to travel without any interruption at a speed 3 times greater than its rate of transmission in air. The signals are received by small tanks containing microphones, placed on the inside of the hull of the vessel on the port and starboard sides below the water level. These tanks, which may be termed the 'ears' of the ship, are connected to a direction indicator on the navigating bridge by ordinary telephonic cable. By moving the switch on the indicator box to port, the port 'ear' only is in operation. By changing the switch to starboard, the starboard 'ear' commences its work. Assuming the bell to be on the port side of the ship, it is only by that 'ear' sounds are received. Should, however, the bell be dead ahead, the sound will be heard equally by both 'ears'. The signals, therefore, not only give warning of the ship's proximity to a point of danger, but also assist her progress in a fog, as the navigating officer can by their aid tell with more certainty where the ship is located.

Welin double-acting Boat Davits.

· WHITE · STAR · LINE ·

· DIAGRAM · FOR · USE · OF · BOATS' · CREWS ·

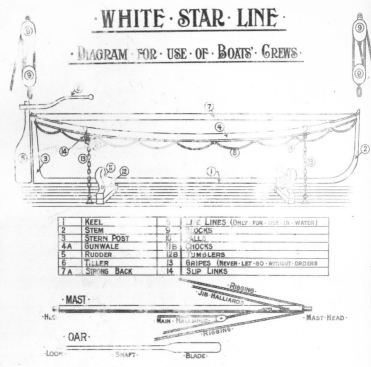

1	KEEL	8	LIFE LINES (ONLY · FOR · USE · IN · WATER)
2	STEM	9	BLOCKS
3	STERN POST	10	FALLS
4A	GUNWALE	11B	CHOCKS
5	RUDDER	12B	TUMBLERS
6	TILLER	13	GRIPES (NEVER · LET · GO · WITHOUT · ORDERS
7A	STRONG BACK	14	SLIP LINKS

· MAST ·

· OAR ·

LOOM · SHAFT · BLADE ·

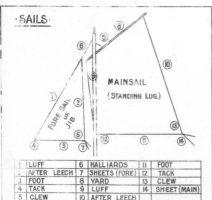

· SAILS ·

MAINSAIL
(STANDING LUG.)

FORE SAIL or JIB

1	LUFF	6	HALLIARDS	11	FOOT
2	AFTER LEECH	7	SHEETS (FORE)	12	TACK
3	FOOT	8	YARD	13	CLEW
4	TACK	9	LUFF	14	SHEET (MAIN)
5	CLEW	10	AFTER LEECH		

· TO · AVOID · ACCIDENTS ·

NEVER · LET · GO · ANYTHING · UNTIL · ORDERED TO · DO · SO · BY · THE · OFFICER · IN · CHARGE

DO · NOT · ATTEMPT · TO · SWING · A · BOAT · INTO POSITION · BY · HAULING · ON · THE · LIFE · LINES THESE · ARE · ONLY · INTENDED · TO · SUPPORT SWIMMERS · WHEN · BOAT · IS · AFLOAT.

WHEN · WORKING · THE · WELIN · DAVIT · **NEVER LET · GO · HANDLES** · UNTIL · YOU · RECEIVE · THE · ORDER 'UNSHIP · HANDLES'

REFRAIN · FROM · CHATTERING · WHEN · AT STATIONS, IT · DISTRACTS · ATTENTION · FROM · WHAT IS · GOING · ON · AROUND · YOU. KEEP · YOUR · EARS OPEN · FOR · ORDERS.

MAKE · YOURSELF · THOROUGHLY · FAMILIAR WITH · THE · WORKING · PARTS · OF · YOUR · BOAT AND · LAUNCHING · GEAR, · THEIR · NAMES · AND USES. DO · NOT · BE · BACKWARD · IN · ASKING QUESTIONS · IF · DOUBTFUL · OF · ANYTHING.

Ships' Flags

Particular attention is to be devoted to the arrangement of flags so that when flying they will have a symmetrical appearance. The flags should be evenly spaced and the same number of square flags between pendants. Since there are only two burgees in the International Code the best position for them is at each end of the line. The appearance of a string of flags is often completely spoilt by the line sagging in the middle. It is hard to avoid such an occurrence when flags are merely toggled together, but may be successfully overcome by fitting dressing lines. These lines may be made of light wire or small manila. The flags are seized to the lines, the middle of the hoist being secured to the line with a whipping of sailmaker's twine. When seizing the flags to the line, the utmost care is to be taken to ensure the flags are evenly spaced; holidays between flags spoil the effect. If manila rope is used, be sure the rope is thoroughly stretched before setting up otherwise sagging is sure to come.

The order of flags may be left to the discretion of the responsible officer. The ensign is carried in its proper place. No ensigns of any kind are to be used in dressing lines.

- Brown's Signalling, 1908

SHIP'S SIGNAL The ship's Distinguishing Signal, used to identify her to another vessel or shore station during an exchange of signals, has been assigned as HVMP.

THE BLUE ENSIGN This flag is flown from the ensign staff at the stern during daylight hours to display the ship's nationality. *Titanic* is permitted to fly the Blue Ensign since her Captain, E. J. Smith, as a Commander, R.N.R., holds Admiralty Warrant No. 690. At least 10 ratings or officers of the ship's company are also members of the Royal Naval Reserve. The Blue or Red Ensign is also flown from the foremast when the ship is dressed in British waters.

THE AMERICAN AND FRENCH ENSIGNS *Titanic* flies the famous Stars and Stripes as a courtesy flag at the ship's foremast. The American ensign is to be flown at Southampton, and will continue to fly for the duration of the ship's passage down Southampton water. The French ensign will be flown entering Cherbourg, and for the entire time in port until sunset. The American ensign

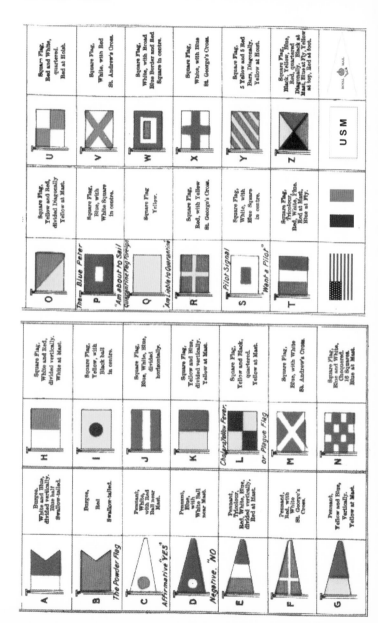

A	Burgee, White and Blue, divided vertically. Swallow-tailed.
B	Burgee, Red Swallow-tailed.
C — The Powder Flag	Pennant, White, with Red Ball near Mast.
C — Affirmative "YES"	
D — Negative. "NO"	Pennant, Blue, with White Ball near Mast.
E	Pennant, Tricolour, Red, White, Blue, divided vertically. Red at Mast.
F	Pennant, Red, with White St. George's Cross.
G	Pennant, Yellow and Blue, vertically. Yellow at Mast.
H	Square Flag, White and Red, divided vertically. White at Mast.
I	Square Flag, Yellow, with Black ball in centre.
J	Square Flag, Blue, White, Blue, divided horizontally.
K	Square Flag, Yellow and Blue, divided vertically. Yellow at Mast.
L — Cholera, Yellow Fever, or Plague Flag	Square Flag, Yellow and Black, quartered. Yellow at Mast.
M	Square Flag, Blue, with White St. Andrew's Cross.
N	Square Flag, Blue and White, Chequered. 16 Squares. Blue at Mast.
O	Square Flag, Yellow and Red, divided Diagonally. Yellow at Mast.
P — The Blue Peter. "Am about to Sail"	Square Flag, Blue, with White Square in centre.
Q — Quarantine Flag. "Am liable to Quarantine"	Square Flag, Yellow.
R	Square Flag, Red, with Yellow St. George's Cross.
S — Pilot Signal. "Want a Pilot"	Square Flag, White, with Blue Square in centre.
T	Square Flag, Tricolour, Red, White, Blue. Red at Mast, Blue at Fly.
U	Square Flag, Red and White, quartered. Red at Hoist.
V	Square Flag, White, with Red St. Andrew's Cross.
W	Square Flag, White, with Broad Blue Border and Red Square in centre.
X	Square Flag, White, with Blue St. George's Cross.
Y	Square Flag, 5 Yellow and 5 Red Bars, Diagonally. Yellow at Hoist.
Z	Square Flag, Black, Yellow, Blue, Red, quartered Diagonally. Black at Mast, Blue at Fly, Yellow at top, Red at foot.

is again to be flown entering Queenstown and for the duration of her time in harbour. Upon entering New York, the American ensign will be raised a third time and flown daily from 8 a.m. to sunset during *Titanic*'s time in port.

THE WHITE STAR LINE HOUSE FLAG The signature tapered swallowtail flag of the White Star Line is the house flag, flown from the flag halyards at the top of the mainmast from 8 a.m. to sunset.

MAIL FLAGS As befits such a grand ship, *Titanic* has been bestowed the honour of carrier of the mails under contract to the governments of Great Britain and the United States. The Royal Mail pennant and U.S. Mail flag fly from the second halyard at the mainmast, at the height of the backstays where they meet the mast.

PILOT JACK The Pilot or Merchant Jack, consisting of the Union Jack with a white border (the white border being one-third the breadth of the Union Jack) is flown only on ceremonial occasions when the ship is dressed with flag lines.

BLUE PETER This signal flag is hoisted to indicate an intention to sail. It can be flown from one of the signal halyards off the bridge or from the second halyard at the foremast (the first being already in use for the courtesy ensign).

INDEX

IMAGE CREDITS & REFERENCES

The editor and publisher would like to thank the following sources for the use of illustrations as noted in brackets: The Bridgeman Art Library (p2); The Mary Evans Picture Library (pp7, 59, 60-61, 64-65, 67, 68, 69, 77 [both], 78, 110); Merseyside Maritime Museum/National Museums Liverpool (p122); National Maritime Museum, Greenwich (pp107-109: F5245, 125: F2657); P&O (pp72, 73, 74); Southampton City Council Arts & Heritage (p99), United States Library of Congress (pp20, 26). All other images © CPL or Public Domain. Anova Books Ltd. is committed to respecting the intellectual property rights of others. We have therefore taken all reasonable efforts to ensure that the reproduction of all images is done with the full consent of the copyright holders. If you are aware of any unintentional omissions, please contact the company so that any necessary corrections can be made for future editions of this book.

BIBLIOGRAPHY: *A Night to Remember*, Lord (Penguin, 1978); *Anatomy of the Titanic*, McCluskie (PRC, 1998); *Last Dinner on the Titanic: Menus and Recipes from the Great Liner*, Archbold & McCauley (Hyperion, 1997); *The Birth of the Titanic*, McCaughan (McGill-Queens University Press, 1999); *The History of the White Star Line*, Gardiner (Ian Allan, 2001); *Titanic*, Thresh (Bison Group, 1992); *Titanic: A Journey Through Time*, Eaton & Haas (PSL, 1999); *Titanic and her sisters Olympic and Britannic*, McCluskie, Sharpe, Marriott (PRC, 2002); *Titanic From Rare Historical Reports*, Boyd-Smith (Brooks, 1997); *Titanic: Triumph and Tragedy*, Eaton & Haas (PSL, 1986).

SOURCE MATERIAL: *Brown's Signalling*, 1908; National Maritime Museum, Greenwich, Manuscripts Collection: LMR 11/12/13, LMQ 1/13/18, LMQ 1/7, LMQ 7/9, *The Shipbuilder*, "Olympic and Titanic" Special Number, Vol. VI, Midsummer, 1911; Ulster Folk & Transport Museum: 'White Star Line Olympic & Titanic' brochure, May 1911; 'White Star Triple-Screw Steamers Olympic and Titanic', facsimile reproduction by the Titanic Historical Society, Inc.

Compilation and Preface © John Blake 2011
Volume © Conway 2011

First published in Great Britain in 2011 by
Conway
an imprint of Anova Books Company Ltd.
10 Southcombe Street
London W14 0RA
www.anovabooks.com
www.conwaypublishing.com

Published and distributed in the United States of America and Canada by the Naval Institute Press, 291 Wood Road, Annapolis, Maryland 21402-5034
www.nip.org

LOC number 2011933322

ISBN 978-1-59114-862-3

Printed and bound in China